CHINA'S GREEN ENERGY AND ENVIRONMENTAL POLICIES

HEARING

BEFORE THE

U.S.-CHINA ECONOMIC AND SECURITY
REVIEW COMMISSION

ONE HUNDRED ELEVENTH CONGRESS

SECOND SESSION

April 8, 2010

Printed for use of the
United States-China Economic and Security Review Commission
Available via the World Wide Web: www.uscc.gov

UNITED STATES-CHINA ECONOMIC AND SECURITY REVIEW COMMISSION
WASHINGTON : May 2010

U.S.-CHINA ECONOMIC AND SECURITY REVIEW COMMISSION

DANIEL M. SLANE, *Chairman*
CAROLYN BARTHOLOMEW, *Vice Chairman*

Commissioners:

DANIEL BLUMENTHAL   Hon. WILLIAM A. REINSCH
PETER T.R. BROOKES   DENNIS C. SHEA
ROBIN CLEVELAND   PETER VIDENIEKS
JEFFREY FIEDLER   MICHAEL R. WESSEL
Hon. PATRICK A. MULLOY   LARRY M.WORTZEL

MICHAEL R. DANIS, *Executive Director*
KATHLEEN J. MICHELS, *Associate Director*

The Commission was created on October 30, 2000 by the Floyd D. Spence National Defense Authorization Act for 2001 § 1238, Public Law No. 106-398, 114 STAT. 1654A-334 (2000) (codified at 22 U.S.C.§ 7002 (2001), as amended by the Treasury and General Government Appropriations Act for 2002 § 645 (regarding employment status of staff) & § 648 (regarding changing annual report due date from March to June), Public Law No. 107-67, 115 STAT. 514 (Nov. 12, 2001); as amended by Division P of the "Consolidated Appropriations Resolution, 2003," Pub L. No. 108-7 (Feb. 20, 2003) (regarding Commission name change, terms of Commissioners, and responsibilities of Commission); as amended by Public Law No. 109-108 (H.R. 2862) (Nov. 22, 2005) (regarding responsibilities of Commission and applicability of FACA); as amended by Division J of the "Consolidated Appropriations Act, 2008," Public Law No. 110-161 (December 26, 2007) (regarding responsibilities of the Commission, and changing the Annual Report due date from June to December).

The Commission's full charter is available at www.uscc.gov.

ii

May 3, 2010

The Honorable ROBERT C. BYRD
President Pro Tempore of the Senate, Washington, D.C. 20510
The Honorable NANCY PELOSI
Speaker of the House of Representatives, Washington, D.C. 20515

DEAR SENATOR BYRD AND SPEAKER PELOSI:

We are pleased to transmit the record of our April 8, 2010 public hearing on *"China's Environmental and Green Energy Policies."* The Floyd D. Spence National Defense Authorization Act (amended by Pub. L. No. 109-108, section 635(a)) provides the basis for this hearing.

Assistant Secretary of Energy for Policy and International Affairs, **David Sandalow**, provided the Commission with the Obama Administration's perspective. Assistant Secretary Sandalow noted that China is investing heavily in clean energy and unless the United States makes similar investments, "there is every chance that China … will shoot right past [the United States] in the years ahead." Nonetheless, Assistant Secretary Sandalow affirmed that the two countries should leverage each other's comparative advantage and cooperate more broadly on clean energy technologies. Submitting written testimony, Assistant Administrator for the Office of International and Tribal Affairs at the U.S. Environmental Protection Agency, **Michelle DePass**, detailed numerous policies that Beijing is using to improve China's environmental standards. However, she cautioned that insufficient access to reliable environmental data in China makes it difficult to confirm the effectiveness of these policies.

Expert witnesses detailed China's recent domestic environmental and clean energy policies. Dr. **Jennifer Turner**, Director of the China Environment Forum at the Woodrow Wilson Center, testified that Beijing has enacted policies which "focus on the renewable and energy efficiency sectors to help supply the country's huge energy consumption, stem severe air pollution problems, and create jobs." According to Mr. **Thomas Howell**, Partner at Dewey & LeBoeuf LLP, many of these measures are "buy China" policies that prevent U.S. companies from entering one of the world's most dynamic markets for green products. Dr. **Stephen Hammer**, Executive Director of the Energy Smart Cities Initiative for the Joint U.S.-China Collaboration on Clean Energy, stated that despite these strong national policies, many local authorities in China have difficulties implementing them due to a lack of financing and a heavy emphasis on ensuring economic growth.

Witnesses also provided testimony on China's activities in international climate negotiations, such as the Copenhagen climate summit in December 2009. Mr. **Rob Bradley,** Director of the International Climate Policy Initiative at the World Resources Institute, noted that although the media focused on disagreements between the United States and China at Copenhagen, U.S. negotiators actually achieved some meaningful goals. Namely, China for the first time committed to a numerical target for reducing carbon emissions and agreed to join an international system for reporting emissions. Dr. **Elizabeth Economy**, Director of Asia Studies at the Council on Foreign Relations, asserted that at Copenhagen the Chinese government was "uncertain as to whether it should seek to retain its position as a large, successful developing country or assert its role as a global power." However, Ms. **Angel Hsu**, a Doctoral candidate at Yale University who attended the summit, stated, "China is still looking, first and foremost, toward the United States for leadership on climate change."

Panelists agreed that despite differences on policies, the United States and China should cooperate on mutually beneficial clean energy programs. Mr. **Dennis Bracy**, Chief Executive Officer of the US-China Clean Energy Forum, testified that the United States should implement a comprehensive plan of action for cooperating on clean energy projects. Mr. **L. Cartan Sumner, Jr.**, Vice President of International Government Relations at Peabody Energy, highlighted what the private sector is doing to foster this type of cooperation, such as the clean coal projects that his company is supporting in China. Mr. **Albert Tramposch**, Deputy Executive Director of the American Intellectual Property Law Association, asserted that when engaging in cooperation, the U.S. government and industry must promote "adequate and effective protection ... of [U.S.] intellectual property rights."

Thank you for your consideration of this summary of the Commission's hearing. We note that the prepared statements submitted by the witnesses are now available on the Commission's website at www.uscc.gov. The full transcript of the hearing will be available shortly.

Members of the Commission are also available to provide more detailed briefings. We hope these materials will be helpful to the Congress as it continues its assessment of U.S.-China relations and their impact on U.S. security. As required by our statutory mandate, the Commission will examine in greater depth these and other issues in its Annual Report that will be submitted to Congress in November 2010. Should you have any questions, please ask your staff to contact Jonathan Weston, the Commission's Congressional Liaison, at (202) 624-1487.

Sincerely yours,

Daniel M. Slane
Chairman

Carolyn Bartholomew
Vice Chairman

cc: Members of Congress and Congressional Staff

CONTENTS

———

THURSDAY, APRIL 8, 2010

CHINA'S GREEN ENERGY AND ENVIRONMENTAL POLICIES

PANEL I: ADMINISTRATION PERSPECTIVES

PANEL II: CHINA'S DOMESTIC ENVIRONMENTAL POLICIES

PANEL III: CHINA'S INTERNATIONAL ENVIRONMENTAL POLICIES

PANEL IV: U.S.-CHINA COOPERATION ON GREEN ENERGY

ADDITIONAL MATERIAL SUPPLIED FOR THE RECORD

PUBLIC COMMENT SUBMITTED FOR THE RECORD

CHINA'S GREEN ENERGY AND ENVIRONMENTAL POLICIES

———

THURSDAY, April 8, 2010

U.S.-CHINA ECONOMIC AND SECURITY REVIEW COMMISSION
Washington, D.C.

The Commission met in Room 562, Dirksen Senate Office Building, Washington, D.C. at 9:02 a.m., Chairman Daniel M. Slane, and Commissioners William A. Reinsch and Dennis C. Shea (Hearing Co-chairs), presiding.

OPENING REMARKS OF COMMISSIONER WILLIAM A. REINSCH, HEARING COCHAIR

HEARING CO-CHAIR REINSCH: Good morning, everyone. Welcome to the Commission's fourth hearing for 2010. Today, we're going to examine China's domestic and international clean energy policies. In addition, we will look at the potential for cooperation or competition between the United States and China on climate change and clean energy.

As a result of decades of rapid economic growth and industrialization, China has become one of the world's top energy consumers and the largest emitter of greenhouse gases. In order to curb the resulting environmental damage, Chinese leaders have put in place a number of plans and directives with a specific focus on developing a low carbon economy.

In 2009, the State Council announced that China will reduce its carbon intensity by 40 to 45 percent over the next ten years. However, China's international actions on climate change have not mirrored its domestic progress. Beijing has refused to allow its domestic carbon reduction targets to be internationally binding. In addition, it has rebuffed attempts to make its environmental data subject to independent verification.

Finally, China continues to insist that it is a developing nation that has less responsibility than developed nations to limit its carbon emissions.

To help us better understand these issues, we'll be joined today by a number of experts from the administration, from academia, and the private sector.

In particular, we are pleased to welcome, first, the Honorable David Sandalow, who is Assistant Secretary for Policy and International Affairs at the U.S. Department of Energy, who will present the Administration's views on these issues.

Let me turn Secretary Sandalow and the hearing over to Commissioner Shea now for his opening statement.

OPENING REMARKS OF COMMISSIONER DENNIS C. SHEA
HEARING COCHAIR

HEARING CO-CHAIR SHEA: Thank you, Commissioner Reinsch, and thanks to our witnesses for being here today to help us understand China's clean energy and environmental policies.

As Bill mentioned, today China is in the unusual position of being the world's largest emitter of greenhouse gases while simultaneously at the forefront of building its own world-class clean energy industry. In 2009 alone, the Chinese government spent nearly $35 billion to support its renewable energy sector, almost double what the United States spent.

Because of Chinese government support, China accounts for 60 percent of world use of small-scale hydropower, is first in the world for wind turbine manufacturing, and accounts for nearly 40 percent of all solar cell exports.

As China builds up its own domestic renewable energy industry, it has also adopted policies that disadvantage U.S. clean energy companies seeking to operate and market their products in China. For example, China's "indigenous innovation" policy appears to prevent foreign renewable energy manufacturing companies from qualifying for government-funded projects. We hope to explore these barriers to competition in one of our panels today.

China's negotiating stance at international environmental summits may impact the United States as well. During this hearing, we hope to get a fuller understanding of China's behavior at the 2009 Copenhagen conference. What really happened at Copenhagen and what does this portend for future international agreements on climate change? Is China's partnership with the BASIC group of nations a model for future action? And is China's role at Copenhagen indicative of a more confident nation on the international stage? We hope that our experts today will address these questions.

Regardless of the differences between Beijing and Washington, bilateral cooperation on clean energy is an area that both countries should continue to embrace. Almost 30 years of collaboration on environmental initiatives have benefitted both the United States and China, as well as the global commons.

One of our goals today is to see how we can expand this cooperation in the future without harming U.S. interests in the process.

PANEL I: ADMINISTRATION PERSPECTIVES

HEARING CO-CHAIR SHEA: In the first panel this morning we'll hear from David Sandalow, Assistant Secretary for Policy and International Affairs for the Department of Energy. Assistant Secretary Sandalow was most recently the Energy and Environment Scholar and a Senior Fellow in the Foreign Studies Program of the Brookings Institution, and the Energy and Climate Change Working Group Chair of the Clinton Global Initiative.

Previously, Mr. Sandalow served as Assistant Secretary of State for Oceans, Environment and Science; Senior Director of Environmental Affairs for the National Security Council; Associate Director for the Global Environment for the White House Council on Environmental Quality; and Executive Vice President of the World Wildlife Fund for the United States.

He has written widely on energy and environmental policy and is a graduate of Yale College and the University of Michigan Law School. Mr. Secretary, we are honored that you could take the time out of your busy schedule today and be with us. You may start your remarks.

STATEMENT OF HON. DAVID SANDALOW, ASSISTANT SECRETARY FOR POLICY AND INTERNATIONAL AFFAIRS, U.S. DEPARTMENT OF ENERGY, WASHINGTON, DC

MR. SANDALOW: I'm honored to be invited. Thank you very much, Commissioner Shea and Commissioner Reinsch, and all the members of the Commission.

Last fall, I was in a car on the eight-lane highway between Beijing and Tianjin, going about 60 miles an hour, when the bullet train came by going over 200 miles an hour. The experience was unforgettable. One instant the train was at our side, and moments later, it was gone. It occurred to me there's a metaphor here. The United States is investing heavily in clean energy. We're getting up to speed and making real progress, but unless we take it up a notch, there's every chance that China and others around the world will shoot right past us in the years ahead.

Today China is investing heavily in clean energy. Today in China some of the world's largest wind farms deliver power to cities over ultra-high- voltage long-distance transmission lines using advanced technologies. Two of three solar water heaters in the world today are located in China, and the government has recently instituted generous new incentives for solar power.

Vehicle fuel economy standards are higher than even our recently strengthened CAFE rules. China is investing heavily in electric vehicle production capacity and infrastructure, shutting down inefficient small coal plants and building a vast rail network for moving people and goods.

What's driving this trend? In part, there are three overarching economy-wide policies that are playing a role in shaping China's clean energy infrastructure:

A clean energy standard mandates that 15 percent of China's primary energy come from non-fossil sources by 2020;

An energy efficiency target mandates that energy intensity, which is energy use per unit of GDP, fall 20 percent below 2005 levels by the end of this year--China had reduced its energy intensity by around 13 percent by July 2009;

And then a carbon target mandating a reduction in carbon intensity of 40 to 45 percent below 2005 levels by 2020 also plays a role.

These economy-wide policies are reinforced by an array of sector and technology-specific policies. Let's look at them in turn.

First, in wind. After doubling capacity from six gigawatts to 12 gigawatts of wind in 2008, China installed more than nine gigawatts in 2009, exceeding its earlier target more than ten years early. Its 2020 target now stands at 30 gigawatts of wind and, reportedly, may soon be raised to 100 gigawatts.

In solar, with around 40 percent of the global market, China is the world's largest supplier of solar photovoltaic panels. Lower global demand due to recent cuts in European feed-in tariffs has seen China try to quickly grow its domestic market, including moving its 2020 solar target forward by nine years.

Transmission. China plans to install 4,000 miles of advanced ultra-high-voltage transmission lines, doubling its network. These lines use up to 30 percent less energy than lower voltage lines. China is installing 1,000 kilovolt lines today; state-of-the-art in the United States is roughly 765 kilovolt.

With vehicles, China has fuel-economy standards that translate to around 36.7 miles per gallon and is considering raising them to over 42 miles per gallon. A Chinese stimulus package included $3 billion in funding for electric vehicle pilot projects in 13 cities.

I've already mentioned high-speed rail. China plans to spend vast sums to expand its railway system by 2020, including high-speed rail.

In nuclear, China only opened its first nuclear plant in 1991, but now has 11 operational reactors, generating about two percent of its electricity. This is still much less than the nuclear share in the United States, but China has 21 new reactors under construction with more scheduled.

With coal, China is the world's largest producer and consumer of coal. And that's a point that's worth emphasizing. Even as we focus on China's clean energy investments, it still remains the world's largest producer and consumer of coal. But to improve efficiency and safety, China has shut down more than 55 gigawatts of small coal plants since 2006. It's also beginning to invest in carbon capture and storage technologies.

So I don't want to emphasize China's investment in clean energy without giving at least equal weight to the extraordinary investment in clean energy happening right here in the United States because here at home, we're also making unprecedented investments in our own transition to a clean energy economy.

In particular, the American Recovery and Reinvestment Act included more than $80 billion of investment for clean energy, the largest one-time investment in U.S. history. At the U.S. Department of Energy, we have the responsibility and opportunity for investing roughly half of this total, hoping to speed economic recovery while creating or saving hundreds of thousands of new jobs.

With this historic down payment, we aim to save billions of dollars improving energy efficiency of our homes and appliances; double renewable energy; transform our transportation sector; build a modern smarter grid; demonstrate that carbon capture and storage can be economical in eight to ten years; and maintain U.S. leadership in science and technology.

Yet, the Recovery Act is just that: a down payment. It alone is not sufficient to drive the kinds of investment we'll need. We must create other incentives including comprehensive clean energy legislation with a price on carbon.

Now, let's talk about the United States and China working together, as two leading investors in clean energy. We are the world's top energy producers, top energy consumers, and leading greenhouse gas emitters. We're also the world's largest markets for clean energy technology. That means as the world transitions to clean energy, we are two countries uniquely positioned to make a real difference.

This transition to clean energy is not a zero-sum game. The United States and China can leverage each other's comparative advantages and bolster our energy security by working together to become more energy efficient and developing new sources of energy. Working together, we can do more than acting alone.

We've spent the last year working with our Chinese counterparts on a broad set of cooperative clean energy initiatives, many of which were announced by President Obama and President Hu Jintao at their Summit last November in Beijing.

These include:

A U.S.-China Clean Energy Research Center which is a $150 million initiative to facilitate joint R&D of clean energy technologies. Our initial focus areas are building energy efficiency, clean coal, and clean vehicles. Last week, Secretary Chu announced the availability of $37.5 million in U.S. government funding over the next five years for this initiative.

Our programs also include: a U.S.-China Electric Vehicles Initiative; U.S.-China Renewable Energy Partnership; a U.S.-China Energy Efficiency Action Plan; a U.S.-China Shale Gas Partnership, one that's been particularly well received with great enthusiasm by U.S. energy companies; and a U.S.-China Energy Cooperation Program, which focuses very much on leveraging private sector resources for doing work on clean energy in China.

As my time is running out, I am happy to answer questions about these. There is much more information about them in my written testimony.

At DOE, we've created a new Office of East Asian Affairs and are hiring five new full-time staff to focus on the implementation of these initiatives. I'm pleased to announce today that Secretary Chu will travel to China at the end of May to advance our overall objectives for clean energy cooperation.

As I said earlier, our work on these topics will be strengthened by passage of comprehensive climate and energy legislation. The world is on the cusp of a clean energy revolution. China is moving forward with clear policies and smart incentives. Whether the United States is a leader or laggard in this revolution depends on the decisions we as a nation make in the months and years ahead.

This concludes my testimony. I greatly appreciate the opportunity to participate in this hearing and am pleased to answer your questions.

[The statement follows:][1]

---

[1] Click here to read the prepared statement of the Honorable David Sandalow.

PANEL I: Discussion, Questions and Answers

HEARING CO-CHAIR SHEA: Thank you very much, Mr. Sandalow, for that testimony, and, again, thank you for taking the time to be with us.

I'm going to use my prerogative as the chair of this panel to ask the first question. The U.S.-China relationship is very complex, and there are many different issues that make up this relationship. We often hear that these issues are linked. For example, you often hear we can't raise the currency issue because we might need the Chinese on North Korea; we can't raise some trade issues because of other parts of the relationship.

I was wondering is U.S.-China cooperation on energy efficiency matters and clean energy, is that part of this web DCS of linkages, can you see it being held hostage to other issues, or do you see it operating on a solely separate track?

MR. SANDALOW: That's a very important question, Commissioner, so thank you for asking it.

Two points about this: first, the United States is committed to moving forward with our cooperation on clean energy. We think it's promising with China. We think it's promising for our own nation; we think it's promising for the bilateral relationship overall, and we think it's promising for the world as a whole. So we're committed to moving forward on it.

A second point is more of a personal reflection because I've worked on these issues for a number of years, including in the government in the 1990s, and I am struck as a government official today at the prominence that these issues have in bilateral relationships. When leaders of nations get together today, including the leaders of U.S. and China, energy issues are the top of the agenda. I think that wasn't always the case if you go back through history, and I think it's one of a number of trends that suggest the enormous potential for making progress in this area.

Another trend on this, I think, is the incredible talent that's going into this area from young people in both our countries. I talk to professors in engineering schools who say that some of their brightest students are now going into the energy area. So I'm quite optimistic about our ability to make progress on these difficult issues over the next couple of decades, in part because of that and in part because of the prominence these issues are getting in bilateral relationships like the one between U.S. and China.

HEARING CO-CHAIR SHEA: Do you think the motivating force in China is not really this concern about global warming, but it's more a concern about, one, our cities and towns are too polluted, and it's creating social instability; this is an economic opportunity for us? And, two, my sense is those are the real driving forces behind what China is doing rather than a broader concern about climate change. What's your take on that?

MR. SANDALOW: Commissioner, I always hesitate to speculate on other people's motives. I can report on what I see and what I hear. What the Chinese have said to us in these discussions is that they are concerned about climate change, concerned about the impacts on their country from the rapid accumulation of greenhouse gases in the atmosphere.

You don't hear in our discussions with China any question about whether or not climate change is real. And we hear concerns, serious concerns, about what it can do to their country. We hear concerns about local pollution, which is terrible in many places in China, and we hear discussion of the economic opportunity for the country. So I think that's what I hear in the discussions.

HEARING CO-CHAIR SHEA: Thank you very much.

Commissioner Wessel.

COMMISSIONER WESSEL: Thank you, Mr. Chairman, and thank you, Secretary Sandalow. I appreciate your being here.

These are turning out to be some of the most important issues that our country faces, and when the President outlined the specifics of the Recovery Act last year, he made clear that the movement towards a clean and green economy was really at the heart of what our economic growth and future should be.

I have to say that both your testimony and what I've seen over the last year in terms of China's activities and its impact here, as well as some of our policies, doesn't lead me to share the President's optimism. I fear that we may be trading dependence on foreign oil for dependence on foreign sources of clean and green technology.

As you well know, a substantial amount of the wind generation capacity that's being installed in the U.S. is coming from offshore, a good portion of that from China. We're going to face the same thing in solar energy.

One of the opening statements identified that China has not necessarily led in the international arena, but appears to be taking more self-interested policy. When you look at the asymmetry in our own policies, the Recovery Act gave unlimited money towards the development of generation of clean and green energy but capped at $2.3 billion the development and the support for the manufacturing capabilities here.

So that, on one hand, you had demand for all of this equipment; you didn't have the support for the supply here.

I went to the Department of Energy two weeks ago to talk about domestic supply chains, and there is not yet an inventory in our own government on what we can do. If the promise of clean and green energy and the jobs it's going to create here is going to come to fruition, what are our bilateral support policies doing?

Are they helping China become a technology leader that's then going to export all that product to the U.S.? What are we going to do to make sure that Americans are benefiting truly here both from the clean and green, as well as the job creation that we all want to occur?

MR. SANDALOW: Commissioner, thank you for these questions, which are extremely important.

You are correct that our capacity in these industries eroded in recent years, and, whereas, in some of these industries, the United States was once a leader, we found ourselves no longer in that position, and that's exactly why the investments under the Recovery Act and the policies proposed by the President and Secretary Chu are so important, to be able to stand up our capacity in that direction.

As you know, the President has proposed to expand some of the Recovery Act programs for the manufacture--

COMMISSIONER WESSEL: The 48C.

MR. SANDALOW: Exactly.

COMMISSIONER WESSEL: Yes.

MR. SANDALOW: Precisely because of the types of reasons you're suggesting. So, I couldn't agree more about the need to expand our domestic production capacity in this area.

I believe that there will always be comparative advantages between nations in general. Engaging with partners will serve both countries well, and so I think we have things to learn from each other, and the United States has things to learn from other countries in this process. We ought to be engaging.

At the same time, we need to be investing heavily in this country to be sure that the jobs are here, and that we can help employ Americans as we stand up this industry. One of the features of much of our investment in clean energy is a lot of these are jobs that can't be outsourced. You can't outsource the retrofitting of a home to make it more clean, or make it more energy efficient. You can't outsource the construction and maintenance on site of wind turbines, that type of thing.

I think there is tremendous job potential in this industry; we've already seen that in the past year under the Recovery Act. We need to take steps like extending the 48C tax credit in order to maximize our potential right here at home.

COMMISSIONER WESSEL: But our policies are cooperative strategies. Again, we all want China to be able to thrive. We want China to be able to address its own internal problems and problems that are affecting the world in terms of the environment. We know that 25 percent of our airborne pollutants on the west coast at times come from China; that we want them to be able to survive and help us survive as well.

But if our technology cooperation is primarily being harvested by China--the American Wind Energy Association is still below 50 percent in terms of supplying domestic needs here.

In solar, we are seeing that the vast majority of the chips, as you know, are coming from China. While there are discussions of production facilities here, they're primarily screwdriver facilities to put the panels together.

Is China harvesting more the gains of our technology cooperation? What can you show to us that says these cooperative strategies are actually going to help Americans in terms of their own economic growth?

MR. SANDALOW: I don't think they are. I think both countries are gaining from this type of work, and what you're pointing to is exactly the reason we need to make the investments here at home so we have the production capacity.

We, the United States, have a strong interest in China's progress in this area--you pointed to one reason, which is air pollution which wafts across the Pacific Ocean and ends up on our shores. Of course, what's happening with the Chinese coal industry could have serious implications for the global climate. It already is having that impact.

So we have an enormous interest in working closely with the Chinese for all kinds of reasons, and as I said before, I think we can learn from each other in this. But at the same time, we need to be, and we are focused on ensuring that Americans benefit, that we employ Americans, that we build up a domestic industry in this area and restore American leadership here.

COMMISSIONER WESSEL: Thank you.

If there's another round of questions, please.

HEARING CO-CHAIR SHEA: Sure. Thank you.

Commissioner Fiedler.

COMMISSIONER FIEDLER: Thank you.

A couple of questions. In previous hearings that we've had, various experts have testified about productive conversations at the national level with the Chinese, and I presume since you represent the federal government that your discussions are with national officials.

What has always been lacking is the connection between national and local implementation in China, the largest obstacle being local officials ignoring national policies and goals for various and sundry reasons. Do you discern any change in that phenomenon?

MR. SANDALOW: Commissioner, you're correct that, as a federal official, my conversations in the past year have been almost exclusively with other federal officials. I haven't had the occasion in my work in the past year to really engage with local officials in China.

I have had conversations with national government officials in China, with ministerial officials, about their work with provinces on local implementation, and they've reported to me fairly serious processes to ensure from their point of view that the local governments are following through on their direction.

In particular, the energy efficiency target, which is part of the current Five-Year Plan, as described to me, was essentially allocated to different provinces, and I may not have exactly the right verb, but each province was told to take a certain piece of that and a process was created to ensure accountability and make sure that provinces were following through.

But I think some of the witnesses who will follow me are probably more expert in this than I am. I know some of them have been working very closely with local officials, and I'd commend you to talk to them. They could probably provide more first-hand experience than I can on that.

COMMISSIONER FIEDLER: I'll do that, to be sure. The question, though, is do you have any independent corroboration of the ministerial statements that they're getting cooperation?

Let me just expand slightly. The careers of local officials have been hitherto dependent upon their meeting economic goals and certain political goals. The integration of environmental goals or energy goals, clean energy goals into that process, seems to--I don't have any independent corroboration that that is a real factor in the promotion of local officials.

I guess it's a nice way of saying that there's all this nice policy discussion, but what's the reality behind it? I mean do you have optimism about that and based on what?

MR. SANDALOW: I think you should ask others more about this. I've had a few conversations about this, and I've been told that there is some work in this area. I've been told that there are promotions based upon this, performance in this area, but I think most important, we're looking for areas that we can have productive mutual partnerships, not necessarily depending upon that type of structure. We're looking for places where American businesses, U.S., Chinese businesses can work productively.

COMMISSIONER FIEDLER: Do you officially or personally buy the developing nation argument that the Chinese make, to excuse themselves from mandatory goals?

MR. SANDALOW: No, you're talking about in the climate negotiations, Commissioner?

COMMISSIONER FIEDLER: Anywhere. They trot that out rather regularly.

MR. SANDALOW: No.

COMMISSIONER FIEDLER: But in your environmental goals.

MR. SANDALOW: No, I mean, well, this has risen most specifically in the climate negotiations recently.

COMMISSIONER FIEDLER: I know.

MR. SANDALOW: And the world cannot solve the climate problem without the Chinese participating and participating as full partners, and, absolutely, the Chinese government needs to take on commitments of the kind that, you know, of equivalent kind to other countries, yes, other major emitters.

COMMISSIONER FIEDLER: One last question. Do intellectual property concerns and trade issues enter into the Energy Department's discussions with the Chinese?

MR. SANDALOW: They do, and I hear from U.S. businesses significant concern about intellectual property protection in China, and a view that it's actually one of the most significant barriers to cooperative work on technology; that is the concern that the Chinese intellectual property protection is quite inadequate. So we do have discussions on that.

The front lines for these discussions within the federal government are other departments--USTR, Commerce Department--but they do absolutely enter into our conversations.

COMMISSIONER FIEDLER: Thank you.

HEARING CO-CHAIR SHEA: Thank you.

I think we're going to hear on the topic you mentioned regarding the goals.

COMMISSIONER FIEDLER: I understand. But we only have him now.

HEARING CO-CHAIR SHEA: Okay. Commissioner Reinsch.

HEARING CO-CHAIR REINSCH: Thank you.

A lot of your testimony was focused on some things the Chinese were doing right. What are they doing wrong?

MR. SANDALOW: I'm very concerned about emissions from Chinese coal plants, in particular, and its impact on the global climate.

Those emissions obviously have significant local health impacts as well, and that's an issue for the Chinese to sort out.

But Chinese are having a significant impact in the global climate right now. Unless those trend lines change, we're in big trouble.

HEARING CO-CHAIR REINSCH: One of the witnesses that we have coming up later is going to be talking about Chinese subsidies in the renewable energy sector. Is that a subject of concern to you and your department?

MR. SANDALOW: The Chinese have a series of policy incentives to promote the deployment of clean energy, which can be very good for the world, so we have approached it more from that frame.

HEARING CO-CHAIR REINSCH: Well, that's a nice transition to my other question, which was looking at U.S. policy and the U.S. initiatives that you cited, and some of which are based on legislation that has already been enacted--there's also pending legislation in the climate change area and also in the energy area. How much is further progress in the United States dependent upon Congressional action and legislation as opposed to how much the Administration can do on its own?

MR. SANDALOW: There's a lot the administration can do on its own based upon previously enacted legislation. I've already talked about the Recovery Act and some of our proposals on that. I think that has tremendous potential, but ultimately comprehensive energy and climate legislation, including a price on carbon, is an essential part of the solution on these issues.

HEARING CO-CHAIR REINSCH: And if we delay a year, two years, three years, what are the consequences? If Congress delays, that is, not--

MR. SANDALOW: No. In my view, it's a big lost opportunity, and I hear from businesses all the time about their desire for a framework, a dependable government regulation, something they know they can count on in the years ahead, and I think the longer we delay with a system to put a price on carbon in this country, the more uncertainty there is, the less clarity for businesses investing in this area.

HEARING CO-CHAIR REINSCH: Thank you.

HEARING CO-CHAIR SHEA: Vice Chair Bartholomew.

VICE CHAIR BARTHOLOMEW: Thanks very much, and, Secretary Sandalow, thanks for appearing here today. Thank you for spending part of your life working in the public sector. Greatly appreciated.

I want to associate myself with Commissioner Fiedler in talking just briefly about compliance. I understand that you do a lot of this at the 30,000 foot level. Obviously the energy issues are closely tied with environmental issues, and when I look back at the success of the environmental movement in the United States, much of it was connected to community activism and to a free press. As you approach these negotiations that take place and break down and take place and break down, how do you deal with these issues of compliance?

It's taking it back down to the level when we know that a number of China's environmental activists, if they cross a line, end up in prison; the press can't report on some of the things that are taking place. So how do you put those two pieces together?

MR. SANDALOW: It's a great question. These human rights issues are obviously enormously important. They're not part of our remit at the Department of Energy.

VICE CHAIR BARTHOLOMEW: Right.

MR. SANDALOW: And anything there, I'd defer to the State Department in the handling of those issues.

In terms of compliance in the energy and environment area, those have not been as directly relevant to our cooperative programs in the Department of Energy as other issues because what we're doing is sharing information, developing market access tools for our businesses, figuring out ways that we can share best practices, that type of thing, and jointly promote research. So the enforcement has not been a big issue there.

The enforcement compliance set of issues is obviously a large issue in the climate negotiations and was much discussed around the Copenhagen discussions in terms of transparency and those types of issues, but in the cooperative programs that I was focusing on in my testimony, they really have not played a major role.

VICE CHAIR BARTHOLOMEW: Okay. Turning to the cooperative programs, the issue of intellectual property rights was raised. Can you just take a few minutes and walk us through how this U.S.-China Clean Energy Research Center will work? What happens to the IP? How do we make sure--

MR. SANDALOW: Yes.

VICE CHAIR BARTHOLOMEW: We've had a fair amount of exposure to scientists over the course of the past years that I've been on this Commission, and they're wonderful and brilliant, innovative, but many of them haven't put a whole lot of thought into the information flow and who's getting what and how we both benefit from this.
So can you walk us through one of these?

MR. SANDALOW: Absolutely, and this is a program that's in progress. This is being launched right now. And so just to back up, this was announced last November, and this is a joint program between the U.S. and China--the U.S. Department of Energy, in particular, and two ministries in China, the Ministry of Science and Technology and the National Energy Administration.

Each country is going to contribute $75 million. In the United States, that's going to be a $37.5 million contribution from the public sector, from the federal government, matched by $37.5 of private contributions. Just last week, the Department of Energy put out a funding opportunity announcement--we call it--inviting proposals from different consortia of companies, universities, National Labs, others, who would like to receive the awards that are available in the federal government, from the federal government for this. As I said in my testimony, it's in three areas: vehicles, coal and buildings.

As part of our solicitation, we've asked for intellectual property plans from these consortia. So we've asked for the rules that these consortia would propose in terms of the protection of intellectual property, and we'll evaluate these as they come in, and see what plans we think make the most sense, and how we can protect intellectual property in this context.

We are committed as a first principle to ensuring that our intellectual property is protected in this arena, and so this is going to be all about making sure that American intellectual property can be protected in this process, but we're going to wait. It's mid-May when these proposals come in. We'll take a look at this over the summer, and we'll see exactly the right way to proceed.

VICE CHAIR BARTHOLOMEW: Thank you.

HEARING CO-CHAIR SHEA: Chairman Slane.

CHAIRMAN SLANE: Thank you, Mr. Secretary, for taking the time to come.

You may have already answered my question, but as a follow-up to Commissioner Wessel's question, the Chinese publicly stated intent is to dominate the world market in green energy technology. This seems to conflict with working together in a cooperative nature. Are you concerned that what we will do is just help them achieve their goal here?

MR. SANDALOW: I'm committed to making sure that we advance American interests in this process, and I think that involves two things. I think it involves investing at home in our own capacity here, and we've already had a discussion about that, but that means Recovery Act investments. That means comprehensive legislation that gives businesses predictability, puts a price on carbon.

But I also think that working together we can accomplish more than acting alone. I think we can share information, learn from each other, and that we have a joint interest in doing this, and so I think as we go forward, we're constantly going to be evaluating where we compete and where we cooperate. But I think we do both.

CHAIRMAN SLANE: This is an industry that requires subsidies in the United States to work. Do you see Congress going down that road? I mean without subsidies, this technology doesn't work.

MR. SANDALOW: This is a big and complicated topic, the conflict of subsidies. Government policies have played a central role in the development of all energy technologies over time including the conventional fossil technologies. So this is beyond the scope of this hearing, I'd say. It's an important topic, but I think it's--let me just say this. It would be incorrect to categorize, kind of say clean energy requires subsidies and other energies don't, other energy forms don't. I think that would be an overly simplistic way of characterizing energy markets and their history over the course of the past several decades.

Government policies, including what are often called subsidies, play a central role in absolutely every type of energy technology today, and they have for years.

CHAIRMAN SLANE: Thank you.

HEARING CO-CHAIR SHEA: Commissioner Cleveland.

COMMISSIONER CLEVELAND: At the risk of sounding like I support subsidies for China, I am particularly interested in carbon capture and storage, which the Chinese have been interested in for some time, as I understand.

MR. SANDALOW: Yes.

COMMISSIONER CLEVELAND: And moving in that direction. So I'm interested, first, in your understanding of the status of those efforts and then how are they going about financing them? There was some discussion at the World Bank awhile ago about offering differential lending prices to incentivize investment in CCS. So I'm interested in how they're going to move forward with it.

Thanks.

MR. SANDALOW: Very important question and thank you for that, Commissioner.

We've had extensive conversations with Chinese ministries in the past year on the topic of CCS. There is a lot of work going on in China on this right now. There is pilot projects that are underway in Beijing, small pilot project, and one being created in or stood up in Shanghai. There's a major effort underway up in the north of China in Ordos in the province there in CCS.

In addition, the Chinese ministries will often talk about not just CCS, carbon capture and storage, but, as they say, CCUS, carbon capture, use and storage, and they're often interested in looking not just at sequestration opportunities, but also utilization strategies: how do you use the carbon to make diesel fuel, for example, or for enhanced oil recovery, other types of ways of capturing economic benefit from the carbon.

On your specific question on financing, others who follow me may have more specific understanding of where the money flows are coming from. I know some Chinese ministries are investing in this. Some of the Chinese power companies are as well. I know Huaneng and Shenhua, two of the major power companies, have been investing resources in this. So there's a variety of different sources for the financing as far as I understand.

HEARING CO-CHAIR SHEA: Okay. Thank you.

Commissioner Videnieks.

COMMISSIONER VIDENIEKS: Good morning, sir. You mentioned this joint research center. You used the word "program," and today's paper, I think, referred to it as a center, but located in existing facilities in both countries. How will it be run? Will both use their existing facilities, will they both specialize? Will there be some overlap or assignment of duties--

MR. SANDALOW: Yes.

COMMISSIONER VIDENIEKS: Will you please comment on that?

MR. SANDALOW: At the very top level, the center will be run by the Secretary of Energy and by his two counterparts in China, the Minister of Science and Technology and the head of the National Energy Administration. That's the equivalent of the board for this.

COMMISSIONER VIDENIEKS: How will it be staffed? MR. SANDALOW: So then underneath that, we will have staff at the Department of Energy running the U.S. side of this, and there will be equivalent staff in each of those two Chinese ministries. We actually have, we are hiring right now at the Department of Energy a director of the U.S.-China Clean Energy Research Center. In fact, our job application just closed for that. So we had a posted application, and we will be hiring from that pool a director of the U.S.-China Clean Energy Research Center.

That person will coordinate work in three different areas: buildings, coal and vehicles. And we're going to give an award to one consortia in each of those areas. So, for example, some combination of a university and a National Lab and some businesses might apply to us for an award, and then we'll make an award to that consortia.

There will be a director of that consortia, and that director would report to the head of the U.S.-China Clean Energy Research Center at the Department of Energy.

COMMISSIONER VIDENIEKS: So basically are there two centers then, one in China and one here, and with a joint leadership?

MR. SANDALOW: There is one center with headquarters in each country and reporting up through a common chain.

COMMISSIONER VIDENIEKS: Okay. So how many people will this joint center—have?

MR. SANDALOW: Yes.

COMMISSIONER VIDENIEKS: How many people will comprise the organization?

MR. SANDALOW: Good question. Don't know the answer to that yet because it's just being established. At the Department of Energy, we intend to staff this very leanly, don't have a lot of extra staff or money for this kind of thing, but we are hiring a director of the U.S-China Clean Energy Research Center, as I said. We'll see what other type of staffing is needed for this.

COMMISSIONER VIDENIEKS: Thank you.

MR. SANDALOW: And then the Chinese ministries will make their own decisions on that, of course. But thank you for the questions.

HEARING CO-CHAIR SHEA: Commissioner Mulloy.

COMMISSIONER MULLOY: Thank you, Mr. Chairman. Thank you for being here, Mr. Sandalow.

As I mentioned to you earlier, as an alumnus of OES at State, I heard great things about your tenure over there so I'm delighted to meet you and have your testimony here today.

Mr. Thomas Howell, who is going to be on a panel later today, was involved in writing a report for the National Foreign Trade Council about China's promotion of renewable energy, electric power, equipment, et cetera.

And that study notes that China was behind, but they're now moving up in the development of these renewable energies, and the study says the development of Chinese industry has benefitted dramatically from government measures favoring procurement of domestically-made equipment, which have ensured the producers a large and growing market for their products.

The report later on points out that the foreign share of China's annual new purchases of wind-powered equipment fell from 75 percent in 2004 to 24 percent in 2008. Some analysts have estimated the foreign share will fall to 15 percent in 2009, five percent in 2010.

So it seems that we're getting essentially squeezed out of that whole renewable energy market in China, and I think the Chinese are saying American companies can participate, but they have to innovate and be part of the transferring technology to be part of that market in China.

Is this correct, what this study alleges? Did Secretary Chu not get criticized by Senator Schumer and some others because DOE was using some of the stimulus money to buy stuff from China, made by the Chinese, compared to what they're doing to us? I just wanted to get your sense of that. Is that a big issue for the administration and how do you think we ought to address it?

MR. SANDALOW: Very important questions, Commissioner. Thank you.

COMMISSIONER MULLOY: Thank you.

MR. SANDALOW: I'm not familiar with the exact numbers that you've recited. But this issue of procurement policy in China is a topic of concern and significant concern for the administration. We are working hard to ensure American businesses the opportunity to compete in China on a fair and level playing field.

Secretary Locke has been vigorous on this and has had significant success, in particular, in the wind market last fall, helping to negotiate arrangements to open up Chinese markets for American wind exporters, and continues to work vigorously in this area.

The President has launched a National Export Initiative which highlights the importance of exports overall for the U.S. economy. We have a specific clean energy part of that initiative. Secretary Locke and Secretary Chu and our departments are committed to working on this broadly and specifically in China.

So, absolutely, this is of significant concern and one that we intend to continue engaging with the Chinese on. I believe that the types of programs that I was discussing can make a difference in helping to build the relationships that will allow these types of export opportunities to develop for American businesses.

And, at least as important as my view on this, this is the view I get from American businesses when I go to Beijing, that they encourage us to participate in these types of programs because they believe, as they tell me, this is the type of thing that will make a difference for them. So it's a very important area.

COMMISSIONER MULLOY: Mr. Chairman, thank you.

HEARING CO-CHAIR SHEA: We told you we were going to get you out by 9:50. We've exceeded that time, so I think we're going to put an end to the grilling. Mr. Secretary, we very much appreciate your coming today.

COMMISSIONER WESSEL: Mr. Chairman, just as a separate question, would we be able to have some questions for the record submitted that the witness would be willing to respond to?

MR. SANDALOW: Absolutely. Delighted, Commissioner.

COMMISSIONER WESSEL: Thank you.

MR. SANDALOW: And let me just say thank you very much for inviting me here. I greatly appreciate the opportunity to engage with you on this. It's a very important topic you're taking up so I appreciate your attention to it.

HEARING CO-CHAIR SHEA: Thank you very much.

We will reconvene at 10:05 for our next panel.

[Whereupon, a short recess was taken.]

PANEL II: CHINA'S DOMESTIC ENVIRONMENTAL POLICIES

HEARING CO-CHAIR REINSCH: Alright. We'll reconvene. Our second panel will examine China's domestic environmental and green energy policies. We're joined by three expert witnesses to help us explore this topic.

Dr. Jennifer Turner is the Director of the China Environment Forum at the Woodrow Wilson Center. In addition to putting on meetings and publications, focusing on a variety of energy and environmental challenges facing China, she has coordinated several research exchange activities in China, the United States and Japan, on international environmental issues. She also serves as editor of the Wilson Center's journal, the China Environment Series.

Next is Tom Howell, a partner at Dewey LeBoeuf, LLP. Mr. Howell has practiced international trade law for 30 years, including litigation, support for international negotiations, and WTO disputes and legislation.

He has published widely on China's industrial and energy sectors, and is one of the authors of an absolutely brilliant paper that was prepared for a very important organization, that Commissioner Mulloy has already mentioned.

Our final witness on this panel is Dr. Stephen Hammer, who is Director of the Energy Smart Cities Initiative with the Joint U.S.-China Collaboration on Clean Energy. He is also a senior advisor at Columbia University's Urban Energy Project.

Dr. Hammer regularly lectures on environmental and energy topics around the U.S., Europe and China. Prior to entering academia, Dr. Hammer was a consultant, advising a wide range of government, non-profit and private organizations on solid waste, sustainability and energy issues.

Thank you all for lending us your time and your talent. We'll have you in the order in which I introduced you. Your written statements are automatically included in the record in full, and we'll ask you each to limit yourselves to seven minutes for an oral presentation.

DR. HAMMER: Three extra would have been great.

HEARING CO-CHAIR REINSCH: Yes. I almost handed you

extra time there.

DR. HAMMER: Yes.

HEARING CO-CHAIR REINSCH: Thank you.

Dr. Turner, go ahead.

STATEMENT OF DR. JENNIFER L. TURNER
DIRECTOR, CHINA ENVIRONMENT FORUM, WOODROW
WILSON CENTER, WASHINGTON, DC

DR. TURNER: Thank you so much for inviting me. It's my second time talking to y'all here.

Actually your theme today is really very much what I do at the Woodrow Wilson Center, which happens to be the best job in D.C., digging into U.S.-China energy and environmental cooperation. In fact, the first publication I did was called "Crouching Suspicions: Hidden Potential."

But also the questions that you were asking Secretary Sandalow about who benefits and how, is extremely tough. In fact, I have a current project that we're doing called "Cooperative Competitors" that's really trying to dig deep into the specifics of, okay, if we cooperate on CCS, smart grid, IGCC, solar, wind, greenhouse gas measurement, what are the benefits? Who benefits and how?

I think you're going to get some hints today in all the different panels, and I definitely won't have all the answers, but I'll try to touch on some of the questions that you all gave me, some of which I think you already know.

The first one I was asked to talk about is the impact of China's industrial policies on the environment, and I think the Commissioners, are very aware that over the years while they had initial progress in improving energy intensity early on in the '80s and '90s, energy intensity grew considerably since 2000 because of urbanization, promotion of steel and cement to supply all these large cities that they were growing.

But also the key is also that China's environmental governance challenges I heard you asking questions about China's local governments, whether or not they enforce and how and why they don't. This is a tough challenge, but I think if you look at how the Chinese government has been behaving in the last five years in the environment and energy sphere, they really are trying to come up with ways of circumventing the local government in passing much more progressive laws.

You know about the investments in clean technologies, and you've been focusing more on the energy, but looking also at the water pollution control law. Water is actually their worst environmental problem. More people are dying from air pollution, but in the long run, more people are going to die and suffer from the water pollution that's happening in China, particularly in rural areas where they have no health care.

So they've redone the water pollution control law, much stricter penalties, and two years ago created the Open Environmental Information Measures. It's kind of a freedom of information act for green, and it's still a bit rough. It's only about two years old, but they have been very open to getting assistance from international NGOs as well as permitting Chinese NGOs to operate in this area.

For example, just this past year, Greenpeace China and a Chinese NGO called Institute for Public and Environmental Affairs did a survey on how well about a hundred or so environmental protection bureaus were doing in responding to open information requests.

Not surprisingly, they did, as the Chinese say, "ma ma hu hu," "horse-horse-tiger-tiger," just kind of so-so. But what's striking is that, first of all, they were able to go do this survey; they released the general information openly, but also gave a lot more detail to the Ministry of Environmental Protection and to the Environmental Protection Bureaus who are concerned and interested in how they can improve their performance.

You do have Greenpeace and the same NGO Institute for Public and Environmental Affairs also using greater information to shine a light on dirty industries to try to push green supply chain activities, and so these kinds of changes in encouraging open information and public participation and environmental decision-making are also important trends to keep in mind--I think in my mind, not just the energy investment.

Coming down the pike, evidently China is looking at carbon taxes, green banking, green credit measures, and so it's not just about overly investing in clean tech.

The bottom up forces. This is where I'm asked to talk a lot. I bring Chinese NGOs to the States, to do research exchanges, have them write for me. I'm very aware of how the Chinese NGO community has been really growing over the past 20 years. They are one of the few really bright lights in the environmental sphere.

In actuality, to my knowledge, only two environmental activists have ever been arrested. There is sometimes some pressure on them, but I've really seen an impressive growth in their capacity, not only doing things on open information, but helping pollution victims get their cases to court, anti-dam campaigns.

There is even one group, the Global Environment Institute, that not only works in rural areas to help in rural and clean energy development, but they're also advising the Chinese government, linking them with officials, on how to better regulate Chinese businesses that are in extractive industries.

So, there is a lot of optimism, but don't forget, too, that even though they don't have NGOs, there is the Chinese public themselves. Expectations have been rising over the past 30 years on their actual right for a clean environment. The green Olympic campaign kind of helped that.

We see about 5,000 large protests a year in China ranging from very violent rural protests where they destroy factories--got to love those ambitious peasants out there, ripping apart factories because the local officials don't respond--but you also have cities, urbanites, using text messaging to organize thousands of people to protest the fact that a public hearing was not held for the siting of a chemical plant.

You have citizen bloggers. You have freelance journalists that will go into areas and do reporting on dirty industries when the local government suppresses their own journalists. I think these are also trends you need to be aware of.

As my time ticks down, I want to highlight the role of international NGOs that have been involved in China, I think, even more consistently and in some ways more broadly than the U.S. government has over these past 30 years since China has been open.

You have groups like Natural Resources Defense Council and Energy Foundation that really have helped the Chinese central government improve their energy and environmental policies, but now the trend for these, the U.S. Foundation and U.S. NGOs, is to go to the local governments for capacity building.

You have projects that are working to help create environmental health and safety academies for factories in Guangdong, greenhouse gas measurements, mechanisms to help two provinces figure out how they can actually do it.

You also have Pacific Environment, a group that works with grassroots activists on water pollution, to build their capacity.

In the Q&A, we can go deeper. I think, though, when you're thinking about where the U.S. needs to engage China, keep in mind that it's not just the U.S. government. We have our NGOs, we have our universities, we have the National Labs, who have long been working there.

Time is up.

{The statement follows:][2]

---

[2] Click here to read the prepared statement of Dr. Jennifer Turner

HEARING CO-CHAIR REINSCH: Mr. Howell.

STATEMENT OF MR. THOMAS R. HOWELL
PARTNER, DEWEY AND LEBOEUF LLP, WASHINGTON, DC

MR. HOWELL: Thank you, Commissioner, and thank you for the mention of the study. I should say at the outset that I'm here on my own behalf, and I'm not speaking on behalf of my firm or its clients, but I would like to summarize some of the findings of the study.

Governments around the world are doing things to promote renewable energy and renewable energy equipment industries. China's effort is singular for a couple of reasons: sheer scale, the amount of resources that are being poured in; the speed at which they're implementing their programs; and they're achieving targets ahead of schedule.

It's a sustained effort, unlike promotion of renewables in Spain and Germany that have been pulled back, as governments have canceled subsidy programs, and so on, so it's not erratic what the Chinese are doing.

And finally, it's important because of the pervasive role the government exercises in the Chinese economy. We're talking about utility companies that buy electricity that are state-owned enterprises. They are buying from energy development companies, wind and solar and so on, selling electricity--who are state-owned enterprises. Those entities buy their equipment from producers of the equipment who are also state-owned enterprises.

The government can influence all of these companies in many ways. They can hire and fire the management; they control the availability of bank financing to them; and so on. So when the government says it has a policy, the state-owned enterprises listen, and that's manifest here.

The study has really a mind-numbing catalogue of government measures the Chinese have taken to promote the renewable energy equipment sector, most notably in the wind sector, which is furthest along.

There have been various forms of financial support, grants, tax breaks, soft loans, VAT rebates, R&D subsidies. There's been subsidies for kilowatt hour produced, et cetera, but by far the most important measures have involved procurement, which basically stipulate in many different ways and many different measures and many different parts of the renewable sector that preferences should be given to Chinese-made equipment. That has guaranteed a market for the new investments that are being made in renewable equipment.

The wind sector, for example, right now, right this moment, is already a $9 billion industry. The Chinese have almost got that market completely locked up at this point, and that's a powerful benefit that the government has guaranteed to them.

Now, recognize that China faces very aggressive goals that they've set for themselves. They have set a target of 20 percent of their energy, their grid-connected energy, will be generated by renewable sources by 2020. Right now, it's three or four percent I think.

They are going to try to cut CO_2 emissions per unit of GDP by 40 to 45 percent by 2020. That means a massive investment in renewable energy, and it also means doing it without the scale of investments in hydropower that they had originally envisioned because of the environmental problems that come out of that.

So the emphasis is increasingly on the so-called "new renewables," which is wind, solar, and biomass. As I've indicated, there's many, many promotional measures the Chinese have implemented. I'd just like to tick off a few of the most important ones.

The National Development Reform Commission has been sponsoring so-called "wind concession projects," which are large wind farms that are built to generate wind power for the electric grid since 2004. It's had a local content and "buy national" policy towards those farms, and increasingly these big wind farms, they're called "Three Gorges Dams in the Air" because they're so big. These are just gargantuan in scale.

One wind farm will produce--the first one that's being built now will produce more electricity than the Three Gorges Dam. It's almost inconceivable to imagine how big these are, and they're increasingly going to be the market in China.

No foreign company has sold equipment to any of these projects since 2005, and it looks like that market is going to be reserved for Chinese-produced wind equipment.

The NDRC in 2005 issued a notice saying no wind farm will be allowed to be built in China that doesn't have 70 percent Chinese equipment in it. Now, this supposedly was rescinded after the JCCT meeting last year, and I believe the impact of that, the market impact, of that rescission is zero. For one thing the foreign companies that compete in that market already exceed the 80 percent local content requirement. Everybody can comply with that so it's not a requirement that has any effect, and they're not selling anything, and that's as a result of other "buy national" preferences that exist.

The NDRC and the Chinese government have indicated since that JCCT meeting that it is the policy of China that "we use Chinese-made equipment in our wind projects."

Also, in 2007, the NDRC issued a Medium and Long-Term Development Plan for Renewable Energy in China, which mandates that the power companies must generate at least eight percent of their electricity from renewable sources by 2020, and what that's done is it's forced every power company to start building wind farms and solar plants, even though, in some cases, they're not yet connected to the grid, because they've got to meet this target. It's caused an explosion in investment in China.

The final measure I'll mention is the stimulus. At the end of 2008, China enacted, it was close to a $600 billion economic stimulus. The government decreed at that point that preference would be given to domestic products--the stimulus spending. And that has ensured a huge investment, and a lot of the stimulus was set aside for renewable energy projects. I think seven or $8 billion. So that has had an enormous impact on the sale of Chinese equipment in China.

I will repeat the numbers that were mentioned earlier. In 2005, the foreign share of the Chinese wind equipment market was 75 percent. This year it will be, my guess is 15 percent, and probably, actually, no, last year, the estimate was 15 percent, and this year will be five percent. In other words, the market is disappearing.

Where the foreigners can sell equipment in China now is in projects that are under 50 megawatts in size. Those are smaller projects. They don't require central government approval, and that is a market still, and because the foreign equipment is by and large superior, the Chinese buyers in many cases choose foreign equipment, and that's where the equipment is being sold now.

The big projects--all the foreigners are out of there. These figures, by the way, are from the China Wind Power Association trade association.

I appreciate the opportunity to highlight some of the findings of the study. This topic is important because United States looks forward to having a vibrant green energy equipment industries, and this is a large market that we and our European friends have been foreclosed from.

[The statement follows:][3]

HEARING CO-CHAIR REINSCH: Thank you.

---

[3] Click here to read the prepared statement of Mr. Thomas R. Howell

Dr. Hammer.

STATEMENT OF DR. STEPHEN A. HAMMER
EXECUTIVE DIRECTOR, ENERGY SMART CITIES INITIATIVE,
JOINT US-CHINA COLLABORATION ON CLEAN ENERGY
NEW YORK, NEW YORK

DR. HAMMER: Thank you very much.

My name is Steve Hammer, and I appreciate the opportunity to appear before this distinguished panel this morning.

I run the Energy Smart Cities Initiative for a Chinese-based NGO known as JUCCE, the Joint U.S.-China Collaboration on Clean Energy. Now, I approach things from a very different perspective when I come to these types of panel discussions because I'm a cities guy. And I view it from the bottom up where most energy is being used, and that's certainly true in China.

I'd like to recap a few points this morning that I think will amplify the point about why viewing this issue from an urban perspective is both helpful and important. Currently, 600 million people in cities in China, and that number will grow by 350 million over the next 15 to 20 years. By 2025, there are likely to be over 200 cities in China that have more than one million people. In the U.S., we have nine. In Europe, there are 35.

A significant portion of China's industrial energy consumption has been driven by the need for concrete and steel to grow China's fast-growing cities. China's urban middle class is increasingly quite Western in their spending habits: buying cars, air conditioners, and computers at levels that will soon approach ours.

Although the Chinese government is promoting improved efficiency standards for all of this technology, overall growth in demand far outstrips these efficiency gains.

And taking all of these facts together, given the country's current urban growth trajectory, McKinsey predicts that by 2030, 20 percent of global energy demand will be consumed in Chinese cities.

Crafting policies to address urban energy use means we look at all of these solutions through a very different lens. Mayors and local governments become much more prominent players in the policy-making picture, and I can report that indeed, there is growing appreciation and awareness of energy and climate topics at the local level across China.

Now, as to Commissioner Fiedler's questions earlier, part of this interest has been driven by central government policies, which are forcing local government to reduce their energy intensity. Action has also been driven by local governments who are concerned about the sheer capacity of the local energy infrastructure to meet this skyrocketing demand.

Finally, there is the pollution question, and pressure is clearly coming from a public which is asking local officials to examine how coal-fired power stations and vehicle emissions can be reduced. The solutions that cities are adopting are varied. Cities are deploying new subways and bus rapid transit systems. They're improving the efficiency of their water delivery and treatment networks. They're promoting the deployment of solar hot water heaters on residential buildings.

We're seeing an increase in the number of initiatives where NGOs are partnering with local governments to promote urban sustainability. We run one of those programs, training mayors on energy solutions that are relevant at the city scale.

The Chinese government actually requires mayors to attend our training programs, and they vary in length from one to ten days. Our next session begins on April 17.

Groups like WWF, the Climate Growth, the Institute for Sustainable Communities, and the Energy Foundation have all established low carbon city programs in China, working collaboratively with local governments to share international best practice.

Chinese mayors are visiting American cities and attending energy and environmental training programs at Columbia, Harvard, Yale and Stanford. I see a high level of receptivity to all of this programming, although naturally there are big issues of how do we translate ideas that work internationally to China's unique political market and policymaking context.

Now, in tackling these issues, Chinese mayors are quite fortunate and they have strong policymaking powers. Very strong in the areas of land use and transport system controls, and they also frequently have partial or full ownership of local energy system assets. Cities are also being encouraged by central government to experiment with new technologies and policies in the expectation that some of these pilot programs would quickly scale up to cities across the country.

It's too early to say how successful these initiatives will be, but it does indicate a growing appreciation that this urban scale perspective is important. But challenges do exist, and let me highlight three this morning:

First, energy efficiency project financing is a problem at the local level. The so-called "Energy Service Company," or ESCO model, that is very common in the West has been very slow to gain traction in China.

Carbon credits have been important, but there are many more opportunities that these project-based instruments simply don't apply to.

Secondly, at the local level, the Five Year Plan tends to trump any orientation towards longer energy planning. When you're talking about revamping the energy system in the city, you must have a decades-long perspective. A Five Year Plan it will make incremental progress, but it won't make the level of progress that we actually need.

The situation is exacerbated by the fact that the average mayor in China only holds office for 2.5 years before they move on to their next post.

Finally, in a situation that parallels fears of American cities, local officials in China consistently express concern that excessive focus on energy and environmental topics will slow local economic growth.

They're expected to, as you noted, deliver that GDP growth regularly, and there are actual report cards that evaluate local official performance, and I believe approximately 70 percent of the 100 point scale are geared towards economic metrics.

I should note that this is not just a China local government phenomenon, however. I could raise many of these same issues when I look at American or European cities. The reality is that urban energy planning is difficult regardless of the locale.

But I conclude by restating the message I started with a few minutes ago, and that's that cities in China are growing at an astonishing rate, and unless we help them grow in a manner that promotes energy efficiency, the implications will be both long-lasting and dire.

Thank you for your attention, and I'm happy to take any questions.

[The statement follows:]

Prepared Statement of Dr. Stephen A. Hammer, Executive Director, Energy Smart Cities Initiative, Joint US-China Collaboration on Clean Energy, New York, New York

Mr. Reinsch, Mr. Shea, and other distinguished members of the US-China Economic and Security Review Commission. Thank you very much for the invitation to join you this morning. It is an honor to be here.

My name is Stephen Hammer, and I am the Executive Director of the Energy Smart Cities Initiative, a project of the Shanghai, Beijing and Washington DC-based NGO known as JUCCCE – the Joint US-China Collaboration on Clean Energy. For the past three years, JUCCCE has been working to change the way China uses and supplies its energy.

I am an urban energy and climate specialist, so my views this morning will likely approach the topic from a decidedly different vantage point from most other speakers today. Before I joined JUCCCE in January I taught and ran a research program at Columbia University focused on energy policymaking in cities. I joined JUCCCE because of what I saw as both the extraordinary opportunity and imperative to work directly with local government officials in China on energy and climate matters.

A brief recap of some basic facts will clarify why I think it is both important and helpful to view China's energy policymaking through an urban lens.

- There are currently roughly 600 million people who live in cities in China, and this number is expected to grow by more than 350 million over the next 15-20 years.
- By 2025, there are likely to be over 200 cities in China with populations exceeding 1 million people. In the US, there are only 9 cities of this size; in Europe, only 35 cities exceed this size threshold.
- McKinsey and Company predicts that by 2025, there will be 40 billion m^2 of new floor space constructed in Chinese cities, requiring 20,000 to 50,000 new skyscrapers over 30 stories tall.
- A significant portion of China's industrial energy consumption has been driven by the need for concrete and steel to construct China's growing cities. Given the country's current urban growth trajectory, this situation will not change any time soon.
- China's growing middle class is increasingly purchasing energy consuming products, ranging from cars to air conditioners to computers. Although the Chinese government is promoting improved efficiency standards for these products, overall growth in demand far outstrips these efficiency gains.
- All told, McKinsey predicts that by 2030, Chinese cities will be responsible for fully 20% of global energy demand

Crafting policies to address this situation means looking at the problem through a different lens. Mayors become more prominent players in the policymaking picture, and in China, I can report that there is growing appreciation and awareness of energy and climate topics at the local level.

Part of this interest has been driven by central government policies forcing local governments to reduce the energy intensity of their cities. Part of this has been driven by concerns of local officials over the adequacy of the local energy infrastructure, including the reliability of energy derived from power plants located far outside of their city.

Part of this has also been driven by local officials trying to address their growing pollution problems, both from coal-fired power plants and from vehicle emissions.

Cities in China are deploying new subway and bus rapid transit systems, pursuing tree planting programs, improving the efficiency of their water delivery and treatment networks, and promoting the deployment of solar hot water heaters on residential rooftops. Local authorities are also working with local businesses to reduce their energy consumption, in some cases going so far as to shut down the least efficient firms altogether.

We're also seeing a jump in the number of initiatives where NGOs partner with local government to promote urban sustainability. JUCCCE runs one of those programs, training mayors on energy solutions relevant at the city scale. The Chinese government requires Mayors from around the country to attend our trainings, which vary in length from 1 to 10 days. I head to Beijing next week for our next session, which is scheduled for April 17th.

Other international NGOs like WWF, the Climate Group, the Institute for Sustainable Communities, and the Energy Foundation have also established low carbon city programs in China, sharing international best practice strategies with local officials around the country. Chinese mayors are visiting their counterparts in the US, and attending energy and environmental training programs at Harvard, Yale, Columbia, and Stanford.

I see a high level of receptivity to this programming, although naturally there are challenges translating ideas that work internationally to China's unique political, government, and market context.

In tackling these issues, mayors in China are fortunate that they tend to have significant policymaking powers, exceeding those of their counterparts here in the west. They have particularly strong land use controls, and often have full or partial ownership of key local energy system assets. Cities are also increasingly being encouraged to experiment with new technologies or policies, in the expectation that successful pilot programs would quickly be deployed at scale in cities across the country.

It is too early to say how successful these initiatives will be, but it does indicate a growing appreciation for how cities must play a role in shaping China's energy future.

At the same time, however, that progress will be challenging. I could talk about many factors, but I will focus my time this morning on three topics.

First, project financing is a problem at the local level, with many local authorities reporting difficulties accessing the capital necessary to make energy efficiency upgrades. In the west, we often rely on Energy Service Companies (ESCOs) to help pay for this work, but that model has been slow to gain traction in China. Carbon instruments have obviously helped finance a great many projects across China, but there are many more opportunities for which these project-based instruments are ill suited.

Second, at the local level, long-term planning tends to take a back seat to the dominant planning paradigm in China, the 5-year plan. This leads local authorities to emphasize strategies that will deliver on 5-year plan commitments or have a quick payback period, rather than projects with a longer time horizon or less tangible benefits. This situation is exacerbated by the fact that the average mayor in China only holds office for 2.5 years before moving onto their next post.

Finally, in a situation that parallels concerns in the US, local officials in China consistently express concern that excessive focus on energy and environmental matters will slow local economic growth. Because local officials are expected to deliver 6-8% GDP growth each year, and because the 'report cards' used to evaluate local official performance are so heavily skewed toward economic indicators, meaningful progress may take some time.

I should emphasize that if you asked me to comment on how local governments in the US are approaching energy and climate matters, I might well say similar things. The reality is that urban energy planning is difficult, regardless of the locale. Many institutional barriers exist that make it difficult to deliver quick progress.

But I conclude by restating the message I started with a few minutes ago: it is at the local level in China where progress *must* be achieved.

Energy use in Chinese cities is growing fast, and will continue to grow for many years to come. Local authorities and provincial and central government officials across China must all work together if they are to tackle this issue in a meaningful way. Other countries can also take action to help Chinese cities do better on energy and climate matters. The Obama administration appears to be quite supportive in this regard, and we are fortunate that mayors across the US are willing to share what they know with their counterparts in China.

Time is running short, however, and as this Commission moves forward, I urge you to keep this urban-focused theme in mind. Cities are growing at a frightening rate in China, and unless we help them grow in a manner that promotes energy efficiency, the implications will be both long lasting and dire.

Thank you for your attention, and I welcome any questions you may have about my comments.

PANEL II: Discussion, Questions and Answers

HEARING CO-CHAIR REINSCH: Thank you, Dr. Hammer, and thank you, all three of you.

Commissioner Wessel.

COMMISSIONER WESSEL: Thank you, Mr. Chairman. Thank all of you for being here. Dr. Turner, I agree with you, you do have one of the best gigs in town. The Wilson Center is a great place for doing the kind of work you're doing with the support, the creativity and the inquisitiveness that surrounds most of the people there. That must be an exciting place to work.

And, unfortunately, I find that I probably have several hours of questions but only five minutes in which to ask them. So I'm going to have to be somewhat exclusive.

Dr. Hammer, I agree completely with what you're saying in terms of the challenges that China faces and the need for them to address that through RES standards or any of a number of other approaches, but listening to Mr. Howell and looking at this through the prism of congressional desire to address the economic challenges we face here, we're not benefiting. We're sharing technology, but we're not getting any of the economic gains.

We've developed most of these technologies--wind, et cetera--but China is excluding us basically from their markets. The average turbine has 8,000 parts, has 250 tons of steel in it. Every ton of steel produced in China produces three times as much carbon as a ton of steel produced here in the U.S. or among Western nations.

So, China's strategies of developing its energy markets in the clean and green area translate into a lost opportunity for the United States and could be, in fact, exacerbating the climate problems there. Our client is Congress. Congress is interested this year, as it goes into an election, of what's going to happen with jobs and how we can promote economic growth here.

With China pursuing a self-interested policy, and--Mr. Howell, correct me if I'm wrong--they're not a participant in the Government Procurement Code under the WTO--we have no bilateral requirement that China is able to source into the U.S. in terms of procurement dollars we're using--what would you tell Congress? Should we worry about China as much as China should, or should we worry more about ourselves?

DR. HAMMER: Whenever I'm in China, I'm constantly meeting American companies who want to do business there, and one of the things--remember, I come from the Joint U.S.-China Collaboration on Clean Energy.

COMMISSIONER WESSEL: I understand, but the support for doing this is waning in Congress, among the American people. They're hearing the promise of all this, but they're not seeing the reality. The Texas wind farm that was talked about, I believe by Commissioner Mulloy earlier--

DR. HAMMER: Uh-huh.

COMMISSIONER WESSEL: --the vast majority of the product going into that are Chinese turbines. So while we'll have some installation jobs, the bulk of the economic benefits, the technology, the long-term jobs, are not being created here.

DR. HAMMER: I think we have to break the issue into different component parts, and again when you turn on the toaster in the morning, you haven't had a lot to do with where that power came from, the type of technology that was employed. If you're the mayor of a city in China, you're at the receiving end of the national grid. You're very focused on the local issues that you're dealing with in terms of environment, in terms of job creation.

The vast majority of Chinese cities have little relationship to where the power stations are located. They tend to be farther west with the population centers on the east; there are clearly power plants in eastern China.

But the mayors really aren't thinking of it in that manner. They're focusing on what are the solutions. They're constantly asking us what the solutions are. Are they institutional solutions where we need to get the process right? Are they technology solutions where we need to import new technologies, new ideas?

And we're trying to bring all of the appropriate answers to local authorities around the country whether they come internally or from the U.S. We have a big focus on trying to bring technology experts, technology companies, from the U.S. to Chinese cities as part of our training.

COMMISSIONER WESSEL: But those technology companies that you want to bring over there aren't able to share in the gains. They're being asked to share their technology, but they're not able to supply.

So the question was asked before about intellectual property, and as you know in the climate change debate, there was a question, as we've had in the AIDS debate, of whether there should be compulsory licensing of green technologies because it should be a public good for the public betterment?

Well, yes, I don't know how you get U.S. tech companies to continue to invest in R&D if they can't get a return on their capital investments.

But put yourself in the frame of a U.S. mayor. As I understand it, we have about a thousand "buy America" policies that have been passed at the local level here over the last year. What about U.S. mayors, community relations experts, et cetera, saying that we only want to buy power from the local grid if it's built, if it's supplied by products that come out of U.S. production efforts? Is that appropriate?

DR. HAMMER: I have to say I approach the issue from a fundamentally different perspective. I'm very focused on how we reduce energy consumption overall. You seem very oriented towards the technology that's powering these power plants, and my argument is--

COMMISSIONER WESSEL: Oh, no. I want the same thing that you do. I want clean and green economy, but I also want us to get the jobs that come with that.

DR. HAMMER: Well, whether it's a district energy system, whether it's redesigning the layout of the streets in Chinese cities, whether it is the green building components, those are opportunities that I see great interest by American companies when they come over.

I'm not dealing with the wind turbine folks--I'll just be honest--so I don't hear their IP concerns. But I do know that the service companies, the design firms, the planners who can come over and help Chinese cities recraft or remake the morphology of how these cities are going to look as they grow, they see tremendous opportunities.

COMMISSIONER WESSEL: Thank you.

HEARING CO-CHAIR REINSCH: Thank you.

Commissioner Shea.

HEARING CO-CHAIR SHEA: Thank you all for being here.

I'm going to recite a couple of facts, and I assume they're correct since I've gotten them from Mr. Howell's testimony, and I just want to put this issue in context.

Coal currently accounts for about 75 percent of China's energy production; correct? Clean coal technologies like sequestration, coal gasification, are relatively new and untested, still in their infancy.

The potential for growth in hydropower in China is limited because of the social problems associated with building large dams. Okay?

We know that the Chinese government has adopted a clean energy standard, mandating that 15 percent of China's primary energy come from non-fossil fuel sources by 2020. It's now nine percent. We're aware of their efficiency and carbon targets, but the fact is the Chinese economy is growing at an enormous rate and one aggregate GDP basis will probably exceed the United States sometime in the early half of this century. You've mentioned, Dr. Hammer, the growth in the size of the cities.

So the total energy pie is increasing enormously, and if I were a realist or maybe a pessimist, I'd say that these measures that China is adopting are very worthwhile, and commendable, but if you look at the trends, you look at the numbers, the picture is not a pretty one, and I was just wondering if you could comment on that and maybe shed some positive light on it if you feel that's appropriate.

DR. TURNER: I've been accused of being the glass-half-full person. Well, you can look at it, and it can seem doom and gloom, but I think what's admirable--over the years, I've worked with a lot of the eco-entrepreneurs in China. It's government, NGO, business, and researchers, not just the NGO folks.

A lot of the policies, these low carbon economy policies, renewable energies and such--McKinsey has said that just looking at CO_2, the current policies in place, not counting all the new carbon intensities, is decreasing new CO_2 emissions by half, and we've seen improvements in SO_2.

Of course, there's the new study that's saying that, well, maybe our data was a little off on some of these others, but in some ways, it's almost like Alice and the Red Queen running as fast as they can and not getting anywhere. But and in some ways I think that is in some ways a kind of progress.

But that is why they are being quite aggressive, and when you look at all these policies and also the openness to really pushing political reform in the environmental and energy sectors so aggressively, I think that it's not a choice for them.

They need to think that they can make this happen, and I think that there are many challenges. We've been talking more about the energy, but really the pollution challenges in the water sector, those are where I think the gains aren't as great.

You want to jump in here for some--their glasses are half full.

MR. HOWELL: Well, I will say that they've been upping the targets in terms of how much of their total energy mix will be renewable. For example, the government witness this morning cited 15 percent non-fossil fuel by 2020. They've actually upped that to 20 percent just in the last couple of months. That's based on the fact they're surpassing their targets in wind, and they're seeing, they're actually upping those targets every couple of months for 2020.

The fact is, though, 20 percent leaves 80 percent that's fossil fuel. Most of that is coal, and if you double the size of the economy by 2020, then that's not a pretty picture. Even if you can have some clean coal technologies introduced, and so on, you have, I guess, the glass is maybe half empty in that side of it.

HEARING CO-CHAIR SHEA: Dr. Hammer.

DR. HAMMER: When you look at issues from a cities' perspective, all you do is run into roadblocks, and this is not a China phenomenon, as I mentioned it. Try and achieve reductions in energy consumption or carbon emissions from cities in the West. It's very, very challenging.

We have a tremendous opportunity. When you're looking at the scale of growth, 350 million people moving or being born in cities in China over the next 20 years, vast amounts of expansion are going to occur. We have the opportunity to shape the future with the decisions that we help them make right now. It is not always about technology. It is about sharing intellectual know-how on the best way to design the city, about the transportation policies that can be effective at reducing the demand for energy consumption.

So, I bring this glass half full that a lot of it is not just technology solutions. It's ideas. It is institutions that we can help them build to address these issues in a meaningful way that will change the trajectory of that demand, but we have to do it now. We have to do it now.

HEARING CO-CHAIR SHEA: Thank you.

HEARING CO-CHAIR REINSCH: Commissioner Fiedler.

COMMISSIONER FIEDLER: Mr. Howell, are the Chinese violating any international agreements when they shut international companies out of the wind farm industry?

MR. HOWELL: We didn't look at that issue as part of this exercise. It wasn't within the scope of the task. I will make some observations, though. When they joined the WTO, the Chinese committed that their state-owned enterprises would procure their supplies on a commercial basis only; that all the decisions would be made on a purely commercial basis.

They also committed that China would not assert that SOE purchases were government procurement because China is not part of the Procurement Agreement. They would be considered just normal purchases, but not government procurement.

Today, China is asserting that SOE purchases of renewable energy equipment is government procurement.

COMMISSIONER FIEDLER: So is it a legal violation?

MR. HOWELL: If they are doing something that is inconsistent with their accession commitments, the answer is yes. Now there's a lot of caveats, though, because WTO legal matters are very complicated. The decisions are 800 pages long; it's very complicated. But the fact is there's an issue there for sure.

And the other issue is, are the SOEs buying on the basis of nationality of the equipment or are they buying on a commercial basis? If they're buying on the basis of a nationality, that's a concern.

Another thing I'll point out is that the stimulus money is arguably a subsidy. There's a rule in the WTO Agreement on Subsidies and Countervailing Measures which prohibits subsidies linked to the purchase of domestic production. The United States actually lost a case not too long ago because we gave subsidies to cotton mills that used--it was conditioned on use of domestic cotton.

So the Chinese are basically conditioning their stimulus money to the developers who are building the wind and solar projects that they are financing with that money on the use of domestically-made equipment. That's an issue; that's a concern.

COMMISSIONER FIEDLER: So I'm taking from this that, arguably, the Chinese are within their rights to do what they're doing?

MR. HOWELL: I think they would certainly argue that. In fact, they are arguing that. They've made public statements to that effect.

COMMISSIONER FIEDLER: Let's assume for the moment, well, you said that WTO might or might not rule. So arguably--I qualified it with arguably--if we were to shut the Chinese out of our wind farm industry, would we be violating any international agreements?

MR. HOWELL: I think I'd give you the same answer.

COMMISSIONER FIEDLER: So the only way to find out is if we were to do it; right?

MR. HOWELL: There's two ways to find out. We could do it and be taken to the WTO by somebody else, the Chinese, and there would be a decision--

COMMISSIONER FIEDLER: We shut the Chinese out, somebody else would take us to the WTO?

MR. HOWELL: The Chinese would--

COMMISSIONER FIEDLER: Right.

MR. HOWELL: --for sure. And or we could take them to the WTO and get a decision--

COMMISSIONER FIEDLER: It seems to me it's only commonsensical, if they're shutting us out, so we shut them out, and let's adjudicate it one way or the other at the WTO on both sides. We take them to WTO; they take us; and we figure out what to do. But right now, everybody is just sitting around there whining about it.

I see, in fact, the Chinese are doing what's in their interest. I'm not critical of them for doing that. I see us not doing what's in our interests. That's what I'm more concerned about in this sense than criticizing the Chinese.

MR. HOWELL: The only entity that can take the Chinese to the

WTO is another government, a member government. That would be our government.

COMMISSIONER FIEDLER: That would be our government again.

MR. HOWELL: That question would have to be directed to the Office of U.S. Trade Representative.

COMMISSIONER FIEDLER: Let me ask Mr. Hammer a question because I don't have much time.

Can you name me the best Chinese city from your point of view with energy efficiency and decision-making and NGO cooperation with the public? Is there a city?

DR. HAMMER: The city of Rizhao is very well known for the environmental policies that have been put into place in the last several years. 99 percent of residential buildings in that city have solar hot water heaters on top.

The difficulty I have when we ask questions like that is compared to whom? The average Chinese city on a per capita basis already consumes far less energy than a Western city. So do we give them credit for that? They are beginning to pilot new technologies. There were four cities selected by the central government to try out smart grid technologies.

COMMISSIONER FIEDLER: Okay. So you actually said it was a dumb question so I'll give you a different question.

VICE CHAIR BARTHOLOMEW: He didn't say that.

COMMISSIONER FIEDLER: Let me ask you a different question. Is an authoritarian structure, political structure, easier to make progress in than a democratic one for energy efficiency?

DR. HAMMER: Yes.

COMMISSIONER FIEDLER: Thank you.

HEARING CO-CHAIR REINSCH: I don't think we're going to recommend that the United States transition to an authoritarian structure; are we?

COMMISSIONER FIEDLER: I'm not taking the questions to Mr. Howell and transferring it to Dr. Hammer.

HEARING CO-CHAIR REINSCH: Commissioner Mulloy.

COMMISSIONER MULLOY: Thank you, Mr. Chairman.

Dr. Turner, Kent Hughes is an old friend, and he sometimes invites me down to programs at the Wilson Center. And he agrees with you that it's the best place in town to work.

Mr. Howell, this is a wonderful report that your firm did for the National Foreign Trade Council. I see that Alan Wolff is a co-author. He is a person that we've had testify before this Commission about industrial policies. His testimony last March and your testimony today and your testimony today are both very helpful along with this report.

Commissioner Fiedler talked about the Government Procurement Agreement (GPA). China is not in the Government Procurement Agreement. They said that they would come in as soon as possible at the time that they joined the WTO. Well, we're now nine years later, and it's still something that is pretty far off on the horizon. But because they're not in the GPA--we have no government procurement obligation to them. So we could cut them out, as far as I could see, of our government procurement market.

In your report you make this point. You say the National Development and Reform Commission in China, which is a high government body, has issued an order that no wind farm can be constructed in China that did not meet the 70 percent local content requirement. That's bad enough because companies here can't access and sell their stuff to these Chinese wind farms.

But I think the bigger problem for what's going on in the United States now and what is impacting our economy and our communities is the outsourcing of jobs. So here's what you say about that:

"This measure that the Chinese have adopted that increased domestic demand for Chinese-made wind equipment induced a number of foreign wind equipment firms to establish manufacturing facilities in China to satisfy the local content requirement."

So here's what I see going on. And I understand that the Chinese nation had a bad 200 years, and they're trying to come back' we understand all that. But here's what they're doing. They are figuring out how to incentivize our market-based corporations to move operations out of this country to China in order to make money for their shareholders, which is all fine and dandy, but we have no counter strategy. Can you comment on that? Am I crazy or is that what you see going on?

MR. HOWELL: No, I've just been nodding my head. The fact is, yes, the local content requirement induces anybody who wants to serve that market to set up local production.

We had the same issue when Europeans did that in their 1992 initiative. They said basically if you want to do business in Europe, you've got to make a certain amount of your products in Europe; it's got to be European made. And that induced investment in Europe.

And, we did the same thing informally with the Japanese, in autos, back in the '70s. We said essentially you're going to have voluntary restraint type restrictions on your exports; you better set up manufacturing facilities in the U.S., and they did.

So the local content is something that, you know, is criticized, but it's also used, and it is a jobs issue. Really, it is a question about where are the jobs going to be? Where is the learning going to be because a lot of times you conduct R&D at these places as well as just production, and do we want to see all that migrating out of the U.S.? I think that's a concern.

COMMISSIONER MULLOY: Yes. I saw in the Washington Post that a company here in Maryland recently moved a plant that was making some kind of solar equipment from Maryland to China. I saw a number of local officials express their concerns about this. But I think we have to see this in a larger context, that they have a strategy, and we don't, and we're suffering from it, and we need to develop a strategy. That's all, I think. Do you agree with that?

MR. HOWELL: Yes, in fact, what I was saying, that they have a sustained policy. You can look back ten years at what they've been doing, and it's pretty consistent. It's like a just unfolding script. And if you look at our renewables policy, we had a lot of government support for renewables in the '70s; then we ended that. We're starting to get back into it again now.

The Spanish have put in a lot of support; they've put a cap on it, at least for now, causing a lot of disruption in the industry. The Germans, the same thing, and you don't see that happening in China. They are basically developing very long-term plans, 15 years, looking 15 years out and putting the resources in place to achieve those plans. I don't think anybody else is doing that, including us.

COMMISSIONER MULLOY: Thank you. Thank you, Mr. Chairman.

HEARING CO-CHAIR REINSCH: Commissioner Slane.

CHAIRMAN SLANE: Thank you.

Mr. Howell, the Bureau of Labor Statistics reports that there are 30 million Americans looking for a full-time job, or 19 percent of our workforce. This is an industry that offers enormous employment opportunities. Would you, if you were in our position, recommend to Congress that we implement the 70 percent rule in the United States?

MR. HOWELL: No, I don't. My view is we should not be taking measures that are inconsistent with what we've committed to do at the international level, and that's in part just because I think countries ought to play by the rules, but also we're probably the most important player in the system. People tend to follow our lead.

I think if we went to a local content, an explicit legal local content requirement, that that would be replicated in other places around the world in ways that would be very disruptive and ultimately harmful. So I would think we'd probably be taken to Geneva for violating our GATT commitments for not giving most favored nation treatment to foreign goods, and we would lose, and I think that would be an unfortunate set of events.

CHAIRMAN SLANE: So do we just suffer and allow others to do it?

MR. HOWELL: I think that we're a big and powerful country, and we have leverage if we choose to use it including in this situation. We have allies who share our concerns. In the past when China has been persuaded that it's doing something, and being persuaded by the U.S. and Japan and the European Union, sometimes acting in concert, that they're doing something that is not consistent with what they've committed to do, they modify their policy, and I think this is an area where perhaps that kind of effort should be considered.

CHAIRMAN SLANE: Thank you.

HEARING CO-CHAIR REINSCH: Commissioner Bartholomew.

VICE CHAIR BARTHOLOMEW: Thanks very much. Thank you to all of our witnesses.

I also want to acknowledge that Dr. Hammer's parents are in the audience and welcome them and thank them both for coming and for raising such a thoughtful son.

I think that of this group here, I'm the sole city dweller, and, Dr. Hammer, as I walked up my street here in Washington, D.C., there was the hum of air conditioners because it's unbearably hot on April 8, and I think our cities are probably running five or ten degrees warmer than even crossing the bridge and going out into the suburbs of D.C..

We really have focused on joint activities on what we are providing for Chinese cities, but I'm interested if there are lessons learned. Recognizing, of course, that Chinese mayors indeed are part of an authoritarian system, and they're Party appointees, and they have powers that American mayors don't have, but are there lessons that are being learned in these exchanges that can be used here in the United States?

That's the first piece of my question. The second piece is, is there any evidence that either we or China are taking some of those lessons learned and using them, say, in African cities or other places that are facing urban challenges--they might be different urban challenges--but are facing urban challenges?

DR. HAMMER: We have begun asking that same question, trying to understand what are the ideas that they are most proud of, that seem to be most effective, and can be translated into a Western political market cultural context.

The striking thing so far is not that they do not exist, but they're very modest. The mayors we have spoken to are very modest about claiming credit for the good ideas that they have implemented. If you ask me in six months, I will have an entire series of case studies that I would be happy to share with you.

One of the ways we are operating our training program is through this knowledge network, through case studies that are profiling, I don't like the term "best practice," but good ideas that are proven to be economically effective, can be implemented in a fast time frame, and we're sharing those with our Chinese colleagues.

This summer, we're going to be pulling together a group of researchers to do the exact same thing, fanning out across Chinese cities, to explore those same ideas so that we can bring them back here, so that we can begin that information and knowledge exchange there.

VICE CHAIR BARTHOLOMEW: I share the concerns of my colleagues about making sure that American companies and American workers benefit out of these things, but there's other kinds of things that can be shared.

Any evidence that any of this is going to be usable across Africa or elsewhere in Asia?

DR. HAMMER: There are many different international consortia that have been set up. A group known as the C40, which is 40 of the largest cities around the world. They get together on a very regular basis sharing ideas at the mayoral and sustainability director level--I'm most familiar with New York City's participation in that because I work closely with the office and city hall. But they're constantly looking at the information they obtain and try and leapfrog the other cities. Say, ah, we like that, but we're going to go one better.

I can say unequivocally that the cities who participate in networks like that benefit mightily from that information sharing, and they take that information home.

There are only two Chinese cities that are participating in the C40. There are very few African cities that are participating in the C40. There are other groups, ICLEI--Local Governments for Sustainability, Metropolis, United Cities and Local Governments--all of whom are trying to promote this international information sharing.

If you go to Germany in May, ICLEI will have their international convention. There will be mayors from around the world who will be sharing their ideas and taking home ideas. We had Mayor Rocky Anderson, former mayor of Salt Lake City, participate in our training program last year. We had Mayor Bloomberg's sustainability coordinator participate in our programming last year.

I spoke to Greg Nickels, former mayor of Seattle, a week ago about possibly coming over and participating next June. There is an eagerness to go visit and learn and bring ideas back, again, translating what is being done, what can be done, into the two very different cultural, political, market context is the big challenge.

VICE CHAIR BARTHOLOMEW: Thanks.

I'm going to change course completely on my question, which is to ask all of our panelists, are we reliant upon Chinese government data to measure the progress that people say is being made?

DR. TURNER: Not completely. There are a lot of partnerships like Lawrence Berkeley National Lab working with Tsinghua and others that are digging into how they really meet their energy intensity goals, and whether the numbers are decreasing, and it appears that they have.

We do see the Labs and also some NGOs are working to help build the capacity of the Chinese to do some of their own measurements, and I think that is a positive sign. And there are those that say that in some areas you can trust some of the Chinese data.

It is striking that, yes, there is that kind of little play around where they might move the monitors in the city, but, in general, a lot of cities are--and maybe you've seen this in your work--that they are actually putting online a lot of the air quality monitors around the city, and our U.S. EPA is working with some of their counterparts on monitoring technology of power plants and their other projects.

So there is quite a lot going on. On one hand, you can say maybe it's just a drop in the bucket, but I know that the Chinese themselves are concerned because when you think that they have committed themselves now internationally that they are going to improve carbon intensity, and so now they are really digging into how are we going to measure this.

World Resource Institutes is working with Institute for Sustainable Communities, also, again, at the local level because, ultimately, those guys up in Beijing, yes, they're up in Beijing, but really getting with the local officials who are increasingly concerned because the pressure is getting greater.

They do have the question about local governments being judged. The energy conservation law was redone a couple years ago, and in that, it says that if provinces do not meet their energy intensity targets, top officials will lose their jobs. So I'm sitting here waiting to see if at the end of this year if we see some people losing their jobs because it is in the law.

VICE CHAIR BARTHOLOMEW: But it also creates an incentive for people to fudge the numbers in order to make sure that they meet their targets.

DR. TURNER: But, you do have the Lawrence Berkeley Lab and others working with their counterparts to try to really push for more truth, and, again, there's a lot more openness in the information. The pressure is building from the top down and the bottom up on these areas.

HEARING CO-CHAIR REINSCH: Thank you.

Commissioner Videnieks.

COMMISSIONER VIDENIEKS: Good morning. A quick question to Mr. Howell. You mentioned Spain a couple of times as having discontinued work in the green area. I read someplace a long time ago that for every green job, there's a loss of 2.5 other jobs.

Is this a problem that's unique primarily to Spain, as far as you know, or would it also apply to U.S. and PRC? I could see green energy, green programs, addressing the pollution problem, but is there a cost in loss of regular jobs? That's my question to the panel.

MR. HOWELL: I'm not sure my answer would be an informed answer. Going back to the China example, if they are going to be replacing coal with wind power, there's probably going to be a net loss of jobs in the coal industry that won't be made up by the green jobs in the wind industry. It doesn't take that many people to run a wind farm. It takes a lot of people to mine coal, and so, in that case, the answer would be yes, and I have no awareness of the situation in Spain, but I gather it would be that kind of calculation that would be made.

COMMISSIONER VIDENIEKS: Thank you.

Anybody else?

DR. TURNER: I would like to note, not to be shameful advertising of my own projects, but in this next year, as I mentioned, I'm digging deeper in each of these different areas of potential energy cooperation. The kinds of questions you're asking are the ones that I want to ask, and besides doing meetings up at the fun Woodrow Wilson Center, we are starting a breakfast series up here on the Hill. I will put anyone on your staff on my mailing list because I will be bringing experts in from around the world--not just the U.S.--also the UK. The UK Embassy has 20 people on the ground working on energy and climate issues in China--CCS.

There's a lot of knowledge, but these questions on jobs, where the benefits are, I'm going to try to dig deep. I think it is a very difficult question that you're asking, but I do want to just note that there's me, and there are other people in my network, who we can try to help you get answers.

COMMISSIONER VIDENIEKS: Dr. Hammer.

DR. HAMMER: Define a green job. That's at the heart of your question, and I would just respond by saying that--and this is one of my favorite statistics in China--in 1980, there were 113 buildings in Shanghai that were taller than eight stories. At the end of 2008, there were 13,100.

A green job can be retrofitting those buildings. Retrofitting those buildings so they become more efficient, installing the windows, installing the energy management systems, upgrading the heating and cooling technologies. Deploying jobs to do that kind of service, that kind of system upgrade is not taking anything away from anybody. It is creating new economic and employment opportunities.

COMMISSIONER VIDENIEKS: Thank you, sir.

HEARING CO-CHAIR REINSCH: Thank you.

I don't have a question, and we're going to have another round because we have a couple of commissioners who do. Let me just make a comment, if I may, and commend the panelists for the consistency and, I think, integrity of your responses, and also a number of the questions, for avoiding the trap that we sometimes fall into here of simultaneously complaining about what the Chinese are doing and then complaining that we're not doing the same thing.

I think the panelists have understood that and have been consistent in their answers, and I appreciate that because I think it helps us get at what's really going on and develop better policy options for ourselves.

Now that said, I have two and maybe a half Commissioners who want to have another round. Is there anybody else? Good. I think if we can do maybe four minutes each, that will be just fine, and we'll start with Commissioner Wessel.

COMMISSIONER WESSEL: First, disagreeing with our esteemed chairman, in the sense that I do want to do what the Chinese are doing if we can't get them to stop what they're doing.

Mr. Howell, let me ask you to elaborate a bit more on some other components of the trade law issue because I think if we simply look at it under the GPA Code, there are certainly questions about the applicability and WTO justiciability. If you look at TRIMs and TRIPS, clearly, in my view, what the Chinese are doing are subject to claims by the U.S., and we could be seeking to take them to the WTO.

On the alternative side, I think if you ask virtually any American whether energy is a national security commodity, they'll point to our troops in the Mideast and elsewhere protecting our interests, that energy is at the core of our defense strategies, that national security is an exclusion under the WTO, and if we treat energy and green energy as a security issue, we can do what we want there and not be subject to WTO disciplines.

So I'd like your response on whether you think if our government is more aggressive in pursuing these issues, whether we can get China to actually open up, or do you think their long-term desires in these areas are so imbedded in their own economic growth, as well as environmental policies, that they'll do what they've done in so many areas and say we're going to continue to have a self-serving policy?

MR. HOWELL: You're talking about kind of an unknown, which

is how could they be influenced to behave in a different way? I can only say that from a historical perspective, they have been induced to do that on occasion. I'm thinking about the semiconductor VAT situation, some of those encryption issues that have been all considered national security issues by the Chinese, but where they've implemented measures that have been challenged--in some cases not a legal challenge--just it's been raised by other governments in a serious way--they've modified their behavior.

COMMISSIONER WESSEL: Do you see any efforts here, though, to challenge them yet?

MR. HOWELL: Not so far. In other words, it was raised at the JCCT as an isolated matter, this 70 percent local content. That's not what I'm talking about.

COMMISSIONER WESSEL: Right.

MR. HOWELL: I'm talking about basically a serious discussion with them about their obligations, which I don't think has happened yet.

COMMISSIONER WESSEL: With the potential for a WTO, filing a 301, and concurrent WTO filing to be made?

MR. HOWELL: That's always there. That's always in the background. I think in a number of cases, the Chinese have looked at the memo and said--actually I think you're right, we got to modify this, which is what happened in the semiconductor VAT case.

The other element of it, though, is what's in China's long-term interest? There are some things they're doing now that arguably are hurting them. The fact that they're using just Chinese equipment means they're not getting as good of an output from their solar and wind farms as they would if they used foreign equipment. That's a price--in some cases, the equipment is not even hooked up to the grid. It's just sitting there because they've met a government capacity target.

It makes no sense in economic terms. They've got size limits on some of the generators, which essentially say nothing under 1,000 megawatts is going to be built in terms of you can't use equipment smaller than that in any wind farm in China. Some of the smaller equipment is more efficient. That's what the Europeans produce. It makes no sense to have a rule like that except to protect the domestic industry.

At some point, somebody in China is going to say we're hurting ourselves in terms of our energy policy because of this protectionism. That can bring them around as well.

COMMISSIONER WESSEL: I haven't yet seen China in any economic area say they're hurting themselves for the reason that you described. I'd welcome that day, but that has yet to happen.

Dr. Turner, a quick question.

HEARING CO-CHAIR REINSCH: Very quick.

COMMISSIONER WESSEL: Very quick. When we allowed China to accede to the WTO by passing PNTR, we did so in part because we believed that U.S. businesses operating in China would be agents for change. As part of collection of data, as well as adherence to Chinese standards, are our companies, in fact, being agents for change? Are they collecting data since they can do that on their own on emissions, et cetera? Are they holding themselves to the standard of their international operations, a lower standard, and are they providing data?

DR. TURNER: When U.S. companies go to China, we are seeing that they tend to bring the cleaner technologies, cleaner operating, and what's a great trend--that I'm glad you gave me this opportunity--is that in addition to Wal-Mart, which makes all the news about trying to green their supply chain, you know, with pressures from Chinese NGOs and also the shareholders back home, we are seeing other U.S. companies and European countries also trying to do the tough work of trying to green their supply chain, and I think that the Chinese government itself is encouraging this.

I think that they are being catalysts for bringing change. What's notable, too, in terms of--I had Duke Energy come and speak a couple months ago, and my first question was why is Duke Energy in China? And realistically as they started talking, they're very interested obviously in IGCC, and you have Cisco and Google and all the big boys going there to try to work on creating the smart grids and the IGCCs.

Duke wants to be there, and Duke says that they really feel--and I've heard this from other companies as well--that China is moving so fast in these clean tech areas that they see them as a laboratory, quick experimentation, so they could bring back better processes and better technologies here.

Again, it's hard to get the actual numbers. What does it mean for jobs? I don't know. I'm trying to dig into that, but I think that there are some really interesting opportunities--I try to open up my thinking beyond the wind farm tussle here, that there's a lot of fascinating things going on in China. There are opportunities, and it's just digging into where, is the question.

HEARING CO-CHAIR REINSCH: Thank you.

Commissioner Fiedler.

COMMISSIONER FIEDLER: Quick question for Dr. Turner. I do agree with you that there is more space for NGOs in China than there has been before, but the question remains how meaningful the space is? So, for example, can you give me an example where an NGO has coordinated a protest, an environmental protest, actually in more than one location simultaneously?

DR. TURNER: Well, the Chinese NGOs, they're quite savvy. A lot of them were initially run by people--

COMMISSIONER FIEDLER: They have to be.

DR. TURNER: --who experienced the Cultural Revolution so they know how not to get arrested. I think in terms of that type of example, in 2004-2005, when Chinese activists organized basically a national campaign about the dams that were being built or planning to be built in Nujiang, in Yunnan, one of China's last wild rivers, and basically no environmental impact assessment had been made, and the question was raised, do we have to dam every gorge in this country? And it was a national campaign.

They pulled in a lot of environmental journalists, who tend to be quite close with a lot of the NGO activists, and put petitions to the government, and Wen Jiabao halted the planning of those dams. Now, today, there is no damming on the main part of the river. The dam-building companies are going a little quieter on the tributaries, and the activists are moving in that way, but when that happened, I sat here thinking, oh, no, that someone is going to be arrested. No one was arrested.

COMMISSIONER FIEDLER: The point of my question was actually in the development of civil society, i.e., workers joining unions, it's okay to have a protest in a single location, but the moment you start talking across lines like one oil worker to another, and so civil society grows a little here, a little there, a little there, until it's linked. So I was just hoping that the environmental community was operating on a different experience than everybody else, and what you're telling me is essentially no.

DR. TURNER: Well, no, this was dozens of environmental groups and journalists across the country, yes.

COMMISSIONER FIEDLER: 2004-2005. This is 2010.

DR. TURNER: Yes, but there's a lot of communication. There are NGOs that come together, for example, the Greenpeace and the IPE coming together to do the survey across a number of provinces.

COMMISSIONER FIEDLER: But there's been no Earth Day equivalent in China; right?

DR. TURNER: They have Earth Day celebrations, and there's a lot of communications.

COMMISSIONER FIEDLER: Yes, but that's just one day that the government sponsors? Helps?

DR. TURNER: There are grassroots groups that do it, but you see Chinese NGOs doing more things particularly at the city level, getting communities together, but a lot of the protests actually, though, is really the people themselves, and which I think individuals themselves, they too are civil society and speaking out for their rights.

And so I think that I even had the head of Greenpeace tell me one time that he feels that it's really the Chinese people themselves who are ultimately going to be the ones that really push for the people's rights, that the NGOs, they remain challenged in terms of that there are no, it's very difficult for them to get funding within China.

Most major NGOs, green groups in China, do receive funding from outside or their international NGO partners, and in the long run, that is a problem.

COMMISSIONER FIEDLER: Thank you.

HEARING CO-CHAIR REINSCH: Thank you very much to the panel. It was very helpful, very interesting, and I will move immediately to the next panel. Thank you.

HEARING CO-CHAIR SHEA: We're going to take a ten-minute break and start the next panel at 11:25.

[Whereupon, a short recess was taken.]

PANEL III: CHINA'S INTERNATIONAL ENVIRONMENTAL POLICIES

HEARING CO-CHAIR SHEA: Good afternoon, everyone. Or good morning, still. Let's see. Our final panel before lunch will explore China's international environmental policies, specifically climate change policies and their implications for the United States.

We would like to welcome Dr. Elizabeth C. Economy, Ms. Angel Hsu, and Mr. Rob Bradley.

Mr. Rob Bradley is Director of the International Climate Policy Initiative at World Resources Institute. In this capacity, he oversees projects on energy efficiency and clean energy technologies. He has spent 13 years consulting for private, public and NGO sector clients on issues such as international climate and environmental policy and innovative financing for renewable energy.

We also have with us today Ms. Angel Hsu, a doctoral student at Yale University whose research focuses on Chinese environmental performance measurement, governance and policy.

Prior to coming to Yale, she was at the World Resources Institute, a non-profit environmental think tank here in Washington, where she helped develop corporate greenhouse gas reporting initiatives in developing countries.

She has a Master of Philosophy degree in Environmental Policy from the University of Cambridge and a B.S. in biology and B.A. in

Political Science from Wake Forest University.

Our final witness for this panel is Dr. Elizabeth C. Economy. She is the C.V. Starr Senior Fellow and Director of Asia Studies at the Council on Foreign Relations.

Dr. Economy has published widely on both Chinese domestic and foreign policy. She's the author of the award-winning book, which I have read, The River Runs Black: The Environmental Challenge to China's Future.

Dr. Economy is a frequent guest on nationally broadcast radio and television programs, has testified before Congress on numerous occasions, and regularly consults for U.S. government agencies and companies.

And we are honored to have all of you here today. I just would like to remind you that your written statements will be submitted for the record, and we ask that you keep your oral statements to seven minutes, and we'll have lots of questions after that.

So, Mr. Bradley, we'll begin with you.

STATEMENT OF MR. ROB BRADLEY
DIRECTOR OF INTERNATIONAL CLIMATE POLICY, WORLD
RESOURCES INSTITUTE, WASHINGTON, DC

MR. BRADLEY: Thank you, Mr. Chairman, for the opportunity to join you this morning to contribute to this important discussion.

My name is Rob Bradley. I'm Director of the World Resources Institute's International Climate Policy Initiative. In response to the questions raised by your Commission, I have submitted a written testimony which I hope can be added to the record.

This morning I would like to highlight a few points from that testimony. First, I want to stress that for all the sound and fury of Copenhagen, the past two years have seen major wins for the United States on climate diplomacy and a huge shift in approach from China.

Second, I want to point to some evidence that China is likely to take its commitment seriously and to touch on its motives in doing so.

Third, I want to make suggestions on U.S. engagement to help ensure that China plays an increasingly positive role on climate and energy policy globally.

So my first point is that despite appearances, the past two years of climate negotiations have been a success story for the United States as far as engagement with China is concerned.

A few years ago, countries such as China were unwilling on principle to even discuss their own emissions until they got a lot richer and saw a lot more action from developed countries. Last year, by contrast, President Hu Jintao announced a national goal of cutting carbon intensity in the Chinese economy by 40 to 45 percent by 2020.

In Copenhagen, China agreed to report its emission numbers and progress on its policies every two years to an international body and to a timely international examination of these data. These are both significant steps and address the key requirements that Congress laid out for its U.S. negotiators.

When you consider that the U.S. was offering China almost nothing in return, this is remarkable progress. So how meaningful are these achievements substantively? On the carbon intensity target, there are a range of analyses. Ours suggest that it will require--meeting that target will require China to implement policies and measures that go significantly beyond their current efforts to curb energy use and deal with emissions.

The new reporting requirements will mean improving information systems in China itself, but recent improvements in Chinese national level energy data have convinced many experts that an assessment of progress in meeting its broad climate goals is already possible, and the U.S. and many U.S. actors, and we'll come back to this I'm sure during the discussion, are working right now in China to build new systems for inventorying emissions and improving reporting and data.

So China has moved significantly. But this will matter only, of course, if it follows through.

My second point is that since Copenhagen, China has shown no sign of walking away from those commitments. Internationally, China and the other major emerging economies have confirmed at head-of-state level that they intend to fully live up to the promises made in the Copenhagen Accord.

Domestically, President Hu has wound up a tough national debate by confirming that the target holds. Policies are being tightened on a range of issues, including on renewable energy targets, and that these suggest that China is intent on following through on the targets that have been announced.

Why is China taking this path? The Commission asked about Chinese motives, which is always a dangerous and difficult thing to speculate on, but many of its reasons will sound familiar. For instance, China is concerned about ensuring future energy security and economic growth. It wants to reduce domestic pollution. It wants to establish itself as a key player in green energy as part of its drive towards a higher value, high technology economy.

Finally, Chinese leaders are worried about the risks that climate change poses to their society. As scientifically trained technocrats, they tend to have a good understanding of the science and of the risks that it presents.

The international discussions have seen China edge into a high profile and sometimes highly uncomfortable role that is comparatively new for them. My guess is that it hasn't always worked out the way that Chinese officials hoped. While they have won some applause, they've taken a lot of criticism, too, but they aren't showing much sign of retreating from that arena.

So what does that mean for Congress? I would highlight three areas for action:

First, the United States should move swiftly to adopt legislation that will meet the emission and finance goals that it set itself in Copenhagen. To the extent that the lack of Chinese action was a reason to refrain, that obstacle is now removed.

By passing legislation, Congress has a great opportunity to cement the commitments that China and others have made and to build the U.S. credibility on the international level that it will otherwise lack.

Second, stay engaged internationally. The administration has achieved impressive negotiating outcomes, but it will continue to look to Congress for ground rules. On issues like reporting finance and the regular assessment of countries' progress, the international rules will make a lot of difference and will need U.S. leadership.

Third, stay engaged bilaterally with China. The U.S. and China have announced a series of bilateral initiatives on important technologies which you've heard about this morning from Secretary Sandalow.

If successful, these will bring down the cost of cutting emissions and create important commercial opportunities for U.S. business. Similarly, the U.S. is deeply engaged in China, building capacity to measure and report progress on meeting climate goals, and both of these areas merit full funding on the grounds of U.S. national interests.

Thank you, and I look forward to your questions.
[The statement follows:][4]

HEARING CO-CHAIR SHEA: Ms. Hsu.

STATEMENT OF MS. ANGEL HSU, DOCTORAL STUDENT YALE UNIVERSITY, NEW HAVEN, CONNECTICUT

MS. HSU: Chairman Shea and Reinsch, and members of the U.S.-China Economic and Security Review Commission, good morning and

---

[4] Click here to read the prepared statement of Mr. Rob Bradley

thank you for giving me this opportunity to participate in today's discussion regarding China's green energy and environmental policies.

Again, my name is Angel Hsu, and I'm a doctoral candidate at Yale University studying Chinese environmental performance measurement, policy and governance. After having the opportunity to attend the U.N. Climate Change Conference in Copenhagen this past December, I've been asked to address China's role in the negotiations and the implications of this experience for China's partnerships with the U.S. and developing nations.

First of all, some deemed Copenhagen a failure because the negotiations fell short of producing a legally binding outcome. Sorry, I just lost my place on my iPad.

MR. BRADLEY: But she does have an iPad.

MS. HSU: I do have an iPad.

VICE CHAIR BARTHOLOMEW: Oh, you have it on that now.

MS. HSU: Yes, let the record reflect--

HEARING CO-CHAIR SHEA: Is that more energy efficient than paper?

MS. HSU: Yes, I didn't want to print paper.

COMMISSIONER FIEDLER: First generation technology.

MS. HSU: Yes. Sorry about that slight glitch. However, this criticism of the Copenhagen Summit only holds if one came in with unrealistic expectations. Careful observers knew far in advance that concluding a new legally binding treaty would not be possible. This limited hope for success was, in large part, due to the lack of domestic climate legislation in the U.S., which left the U.S. in no position to sign on to a full legally binding international agreement.

Given that realistically a legally binding agreement was off the table well before Copenhagen, it's only fair to assess China's role in terms of the degree to which they facilitated the negotiations by playing a constructive role in the resulting Copenhagen Accord.

I make this point because in the aftermath, the notion that China wrecked the Copenhagen deal became one of the most parroted sound bites as people were looking to point fingers and to place blame. However, mainstream media largely glossed over the role a few oil-producing countries, such as Bolivia, Venezuela and Sudan, in addition to Nicaragua and Cuba, who actually refused to sign on to the Copenhagen Accord in the waning hours of the negotiation, and not China, who actually supported a political agreement from the start.

So mindful of this context, I'd like to focus my remarks today on three points:

First, as Mr. Bradley mentioned, China is making significant commitments to address climate change.

Secondly, China is working with international partners to build capacity on measurement, reporting and verification of its domestic policies.

Third, now is the time for the U.S. and China to work together on clean energy and climate change mitigation.

So, first, despite China's reluctance to abandon the Kyoto Protocol, which recognizes different responsibilities for developed and developing countries, China has made significant commitments to address their current and growing contribution to global climate change.

Two weeks prior to the Copenhagen negotiations, China's State Council, the highest policymaking body, announced that they would reduce carbon intensity by 40 to 45 percent by 2020 compared with 2005 levels.

Also some argued that China's pledge was disappointing and didn't really deviate much from a business as usual scenario. This was, in fact, a significant pledge by the top Chinese leadership. This pledge signaled a shift on the part of the Chinese to framing its target directly in terms of carbon intensity instead of energy efficiency, renewable energy or reforestation efforts.

Furthermore, we found out in Copenhagen that the Chinese were making this pledge regardless of financing from the developed world, contrary to common belief leading up to Copenhagen that China would not act without the promise of financial support from developed countries.

Instead, China has adopted a rational scientific approach to climate change. In light of national concerns over energy and food security, drought, changing monsoon patterns, rising sea levels and social stability, the consequences of climate change resonate with both the Chinese leadership and increasingly the Chinese public.

This scientific approach was even reflected when comparing the rosters of the Chinese and U.S. delegations at Copenhagen. While the U.S. brought political representatives, China's delegation consisted primarily of technocrats, academics and scientists. Simply put, China is acting on climate change because they want to.

On to my second point. China is working with international partners to build capacity on measurement, reporting and verification of its domestic policies. Lawrence Berkeley National Laboratory has been partnering with Tsinghua University over the past five years to evaluate many of China's energy conservation programs.

A Chinese NGO, called the Innovation Center for Environment and Transportation, is partnering with the U.S.-based Climate Registry to create China's first voluntary emissions registry. The World

Resources Institute is training Chinese companies to use internationally standardized greenhouse gas accounting tools and methods.

Furthermore, my colleagues and I at the Yale Center for Environmental Law and Policy have been working for the past two years with the Chinese government to systematically measure environmental performance in all 31 Chinese provinces. Our experience has revealed many challenges with Chinese data thus far.

So helping to improve environmental information is an area where the U.S. could play a critical role, which brings me to my final point. Despite their commitments made in Copenhagen and multiple efforts on the ground to implement these actions, China is still looking, first and foremost, to the U.S. for leadership on climate change.

Unfortunately, the United States is already late to the game with respect to green energy and environmental cooperation with China. A colleague of mine recently met with the Ministry of Science and Technology in Beijing, and noted the heavy emphasis the Chinese are currently placing on international cooperation. He told me that the Chinese already have long-standing partnerships with EU nations, several developing countries, and others.

For example, China and Japan also announced before Copenhagen a suite of 42 clean energy and environmental projects. In relation to developing countries, last November, China pledged $10 billion in aid to Africa, which includes the construction of 100 clean energy projects.

Fortunately, while the United States may have shown up late to the game, it's not over yet. All the pieces are in place, as Mr. Bradley mentioned, for the United States and China to work together on clean energy research, energy efficiency, renewable energy, clean coal and carbon capture and sequestration projects, and clean vehicle technology, all of which Presidents Obama and Hu agreed were areas of mutual interest when they met two weeks before Copenhagen in Beijing.

While China already recognizes that the clean energy technology revolution is both a necessity and an opportunity, Thomas Friedman writes that the United States "can't afford to be asleep with an invigorated China wide awake."

According to Friedman, such a "Green Leap Forward" will happen faster and more effectively if China and the United States work together.

Thank you, and I look forward to your questions.
[The statement follows:][5]

HEARING CO-CHAIR SHEA: Dr. Economy. Thank you.

---

[5] Click here to read the prepared statement of Ms. Angel Hsu

STATEMENT OF DR. ELIZABETH ECONOMY
DIRECTOR OF ASIA STUDIES, COUNCIL ON FOREIGN
RELATIONS, NEW YORK, NEW YORK

DR. ECONOMY: Let me begin by thanking the Commission for inviting me here to talk with you about China's climate and clean energy diplomacy.

I would like to highlight three points that I raised in my written testimony:

First, if we look at China's climate diplomacy in an historical context, we will see that it has undergone significant evolution.

Second, this evolution in turn is part of a broader effort on the part of the Chinese leadership to define a new place in the global system.

And third, we should expect to see further evolution in climate diplomacy, particularly in China's efforts to advance a clean energy-focused foreign policy.

To my first point, China was painted as a difficult player at Copenhagen. Having said that, what China did put forth did reflect significant evolution in its climate diplomacy. First, China has for almost 20 years rejected any targets or time tables, voluntary or otherwise, and at Copenhagen, it did set out voluntary targets.

Second, China, also unlike past practice, has indicated its willingness to consider measurement, reporting and verification from the international community--though at least initially only for externally-funded projects--this is something they had refused to do for at least 15 years.

Third, China has always stood first in line for international environmental technology assistance, and at Copenhagen, it gave first rights to the least developing countries, although I think this was a decision made under some duress.

This evolution is important, not only because it shows that pressure and cooperation can work to produce change in China's policy over time, but also because it reflects more broadly on the challenging international space that China now occupies.

China is in a sort of netherworld between being a developing country and a global superpower. It is a country that is both the third-largest economy in the world and yet has a GDP per capita of about 3,500 U.S. dollars.

It has for a long time enjoyed all the rights of a developing country with none of the real responsibilities of a global power. Because of its enormous impact on the world, whether we're talking about greenhouse gas emissions, food and product safety issues, or trade and currency policy, the rest of the world is now unwilling to allow China to escape its obligations as a global power. Copenhagen crystallized for many in the developing world, that China is less and less one of us and more and more one of them.

I don't think China is ready to step up fully to the role of global superpower, and its response to some extent has been to band together with other large developing or mid-size powers on a range of issues.

For example, we see the Shanghai Cooperation Organization, which focuses on energy, security, political reform issues; the BRIC countries on trade; and now the BASIC countries on climate change.

These aren't formal alliance structures that cross the full range of foreign policy issues, but they are potentially an effective means of preventing China from being isolated on any given issue or coming under too much pressure as it stands alone.

Looking forward, the United States will see continued emphasis by China on the BASIC alliance, working through this group not only to establish a uniform climate negotiation strategy but also to align China's interests with the rest of the developing world. China doesn't want to see a repeat of Copenhagen where the developing world was fractured.

A second strand of China's climate diplomacy, again, looking forward, will be the development of clean energy diplomacy. We've all read and heard about China's significant effort in this field of clean industry domestically, as a manufacturer, exporter, and now end-user.

Based on comments from analysts within China's renewable sector, as well as major Chinese development banks, such as the Export-Import Bank, however, it appears that China is going to begin to incorporate clean energy into its broader go-out strategy, something they already do, for example, with large-scale hydropower.

This means incorporating wind farms, for example, into their substantial trade and aid programs in Africa, Southeast Asia, and Latin America. This has several benefits for China. It helps with the problem of overcapacity that they are currently facing in this sector. It gives them a global commercial foothold in the developing world moving forward, and it helps to burnish their reputation globally.

Let me make a few final points on the issue of what China's climate and clean energy diplomacy means for the United States. The evolution in climate diplomacy means that capacity building, cooperation, and pressure all can work together to produce further change in China's position on issues such as further targets or measurement, reporting and verification.

This could be more difficult with the BASIC alliance, but it's not impossible. We've seen, for example, fracturing within the SCO on the issue of Iran, and now China is being brought along, potentially in a new way.

On the clean energy front, the United States ought to be looking closely at its own foreign aid and trade strategy. What are the lessons that we might take away from China's going-out strategy? How can we better support our own clean energy companies' interests with broader U.S. assistance or financing?

Third, we need a clear regulatory and incentive structure to promote the manufacturing and deployment of renewable energies in the United States. It's already happening in local areas within the country, but U.S. companies—often complain all the time that the incentives for doing business in China are simply much greater.

We also need to welcome Chinese investment into this area in the United States. China has significant financial assets, and we should take advantage of their interests in investing in this sector to help us create capital, jobs, and a cleaner environment.

Thank you very much. I welcome your questions.

[The statement follows:][6]

PANEL III: Discussion, Questions and Answers

HEARING CO-CHAIR SHEA: Thank you very much to everyone for their interesting comments.

I'll start with my question first. I know none of you were "in the room," quote-unquote, in Copenhagen, but I think it's fair to say that it was not a positive example of Chinese press relations or perception management. I think, Dr. Economy, you said they were correctly painted as a difficult player; correct? What sort of after-action analysis do you think the Chinese have--I know this is speculation--but have conducted? What lessons do you think they have learned or have taken away from their experience with Copenhagen? I know maybe one possibility would be there's opportunity to work more with this BASIC group of nations on other issues, not--beyond climate change.

But if you could just give me your thoughts about when they all went back to Beijing, maybe the idea was don't bring so many technocrats to the next one, to the next meeting, but what kinds of lessons did they themselves learn from this experience?

DR. ECONOMY: One of the first things the Chinese delegation did when they got back to Beijing was to create a new history of what transpired in Copenhagen. So you saw Premier Wen Jiabao do an

---

[6] **Click here to read the prepared statement of Dr. Elizabeth Economy**

interview, and you saw press releases coming out within China that painted China as a very constructive player and one who was trying to bridge the gap between the developing countries and the advanced industrialized countries.

Soon after Copenhagen, you also saw Chinese representatives meeting with some of the leaders of small island states, which were part of the group that fractured during Copenhagen. There was a statement, for example, with the head of Maldives and Chinese leaders saying we're going to work together on climate change.

In the aftermath of Copenhagen, China tried very quickly to reaffirm its place as a leader of the developing world, and to reunite the developing world.

Again, China is going to be working with the BASIC countries. The group already met in India and they're meeting this month in South Africa. They've planned five or six meetings before Cancun to coordinate their strategy.

Do I think China took away any lessons from Copenhagen? China did bring a substantial foreign policy contingent and He Yafei--who is a member of the Foreign Ministry and was recently assigned to a new post in Switzerland in what some people felt was a serious demotion--was the person who made the negative comments about Todd Stern. Xie Zhenhua, vice-chairman of the National Development and Reform Commission, also was reportedly rude to President Obama. I think there's going to be a discussion within China of how it should better conduct itself in international negotiations.

The real challenge for China, which they're going to find very difficult to change, will be over who has the authority actually to negotiate? Who can change policy midstream? You have the premier of the country, yet the sense was he was not really empowered to do anything new while he was there. Everything China was prepared to give was right up front. After that there wasn't going to be much room for real negotiation moving forward.

Whether or not China can change that touches on a more fundamental question about the way the Chinese government works.

HEARING CO-CHAIR SHEA: Anything else, Mr. Bradley, Ms. Hsu?

MR. BRADLEY: I would endorse Dr. Economy's assessment. I think there was definitely--Copenhagen was a mess. It has brought home a lot of mythology as well as a lot of emotion. A lot of what I spent the last three months doing is essentially therapy sessions for the various participants. People who have thrown 20 years of their lives into trying to create something here have tried to deal emotionally with all of the fallout there.

I think that's certainly part of what's happened in China, too. As with so many things in China, it's the blind guys and the elephant. Here we're trying to patch together, I think, an overall picture from a lot of different perspectives, and so I certainly wouldn't assert that I know what their response is.

But I do think that part of the dynamic was the fact that Western countries, you send senior people, they're politicians, they're very used to the rough and tumble, the sharp elbows of political life, and many of the senior folks in China, they're technocrats, they're insiders. They're much more used to a slightly, a more bureaucratic structure.

The U.S. as part of its negotiating strategy upped the ante right from day one and had a strategy of essentially trying to paint China into a corner as, you know, if you don't play ball with us, particularly on the verification stuff, you're going to come away as the villain, and I think people have been bruised by that.

From the U.S. negotiating perspective, I think it was reasonable for them to say, gosh, this was a really smart strategy, but I think there are, there are going to be pieces of fallout from that that will take some time.

I think the Chinese felt that they had actually come a long, long way in the last couple of years, and I think viewed over a couple of years rather than the two weeks of Copenhagen, that's actually correct. I think in many ways, Copenhagen as something, as a meeting, is something for us to get over so that we can remember that Copenhagen as a two-year process was actually successful and constructive.

HEARING CO-CHAIR SHEA: Thank you.

MS. HSU: Yes. I just wanted to add that it would be really interesting to see in the coming months whether or not China provides more clarity and also international players provide more clarity around the question of what exactly international scrutiny and analysis of Chinese commitments and actions will be.

I think that that's something that there is still a lot of room to work with China on and also the other major developing economies, but I just wanted to also echo Dr. Economy's comments. It was very interesting, from day one, we realized that China knew exactly what chips they were willing to put on the table, and which ones they weren't willing to play, and every Chinese official that I spoke to parroted and harped the same message over and over again.

So it was very interesting to compare their negotiation style with the United States, where you didn't have that same consistent "No, this is only what we're giving." So I thought that that was really interesting.

And then also a lot of the points that Mr. Bradley mentioned as

well.   I completely agree.
          HEARING CO-CHAIR SHEA: Thank you very much.
          Commissioner Wessel.
          COMMISSIONER WESSEL: Thank you all for being here, and
Dr. Economy, like our chair, I also read your book, and as a--
          DR. ECONOMY: I'm going to quiz you guys later.
          COMMISSIONER WESSEL: --former author, I also, as important
potentially, I actually paid for it.
          DR. ECONOMY: Outstanding.
          HEARING CO-CHAIR SHEA: I paid for mine, too.
          DR. ECONOMY: The new edition is coming out this summer.
          COMMISSIONER WESSEL: Ah, well, new forward, okay.
          Two questions, and Dr. Economy, the first one for you because
you raised the issue, although I certainly welcome views by the others,
which is the question about the clean and green and the future for the
U.S. economy and the world economy. There are a lot of people who
are now questioning whether all we're doing is trading our dependence
on foreign oil for dependence on foreign renewable and alternative
generating equipment with China supplying the bulk of that equipment
right now.
          So how do we address that challenge? How do we show the
American people who have been told clean and green is the future, and
they're not seeing the results here in both solar and in wind, the
majority of the products not coming from here?
          The President just announced loan guarantees for nuclear power
generating equipment. We haven't built a reactor in 30 years, but all of
the reactor vessels, most of the containment facilities, are all going to
be coming from offshore, and that's clearly a critical technology.
          Separately, for the other two witnesses, the privilege of selling to
the U.S. consumer should bring with it the responsibility of abiding by
certain standards. We do that as it applies to child labor. We do that
for pharmaceuticals. We want to make sure that products are safe, that
their food, their pharmaceuticals, et cetera.
          The House when it passed its climate change legislation last year
included a border adjustment mechanism that abided by this tenet. It
basically said if you're going to sell here, we expect that the costs of
carbon emissions are going to be imbedded in your product. That if
you're a producer here in the U.S., that's going to be reflected, or if you
are a Chinese, Indian, European, or any other producer, that that carbon
cost is going to be brought into the product sold here as an adjustment
mechanism.
          It doesn't say to China, you have to, or any other any country,
you have to have a U.S. standard for what you do in your own market,

but when you come here, we have a certain standard.

I'd like your responses to that because that, I think, is a critical issue in the U.S. Congress as to whether a border adjustment mechanism is going to be included and how you view that. Dr. Economy?

DR. ECONOMY: Thanks very much.

I had the privilege of listening in on a little bit of the last session so I know this was an issue that was also raised during the session. I think there are two things that I would stress. The first is we need to be very careful because sometimes when Chinese companies coming to do business here, we should welcome that.

Although I don't think it's come to any real fruition yet, a deal announced last fall for a wind farm in Texas received quite a bit of negative attention in the U.S. press.

The problem was that the equipment was going to be coming from China--but the company that was going to be the joint venture partner is listed in NASDAQ--thus China is doing business here, which actually has benefits for pension funds as well as for individual shareholders that have investments in this Chinese company.

When we think about the complexity of the global economic system, there are ways that Chinese companies here actually should be welcomed very directly.

COMMISSIONER WESSEL: And just on that point, as we saw with Japan in the 1980s in some of the trade challenges, Japan addressed that by bringing production here. Toyota, whatever you will.

China is doing that more through assembly facilities. What they're doing in the solar area is they're importing all the products here, and then those are screwdriver facilities here. That's essentially what happened in the wind farm, where it was all Chinese equipment funded by U.S. taxpayers, and that I think a lot of members of Congress, I think, Mr. Schumer was mentioned earlier, a lot of Members of Congress have a real concern about that.

DR. ECONOMY: The Chinese do have financial assets with which to play now, and I think as we're looking forward--there was a big article in the New York Times today about the high tech, high- speed rail coming. So if I were sitting in Governor Schwarzenegger's shoes, I would try to make sure that whatever engineers and laborers and others that China is planning to bring ought to be homegrown.

We don't want to get into a tit for tat where we put up local requirements because the Chinese have a 70 percent local content requirement for wind, which it has now lowered Still, we do need to be very smart about how we structure these deals. China often requires, for example, a level of technology transfer, for example, establishing an R&D center. So we ought to be thinking in these terms of what it is that we can learn from the Chinese and the way that they do business. But it should not be an automatic "we need to fear the Chinese and their investment." We just need to be prepared to bargain hard.

COMMISSIONER WESSEL: Understand. Mr. Bradley, Ms. Hsu.

MR. BRADLEY: Thank you. Two very juicy issues. I'll start with the first. In the 1980s, when computer chips and memory chips were made here in the United States, computers cost $4,000 a piece, and there was a relatively limited market for them, but the U.S. made the whole lot.

During the following 20, 30 years, the manufacturing of those memory chips moved to Taiwan, to Korea, to China. Did that hit the U.S. computer industry? Absolutely not. Because the price of computers came down to 400 bucks instead of 4,000, and that's the only reason we have an Intel today, that we have a Google, that we have a Microsoft, that we have a Hewlett Packard, and that we have Angel's iPad here.

If you look at the back of Angel's iPad, I bet it will say "Assembled in China." China will have got about five bucks of value out of that on a $500 piece of equipment. So I think as we begin, we need to accept that all of these high-tech industries are necessarily going to be global ones with internationally traded components.

Secondly, we've done at WRI together with the Peterson Institute quite a lot of analysis recently on where the value chains break out in sectors like wind energy, like solar, and where those jobs are created.

Overwhelmingly, and this is the message that I think that needs to be brought across, the jobs are created where the market is created. The Europeans, we had some discussion earlier this morning on an earlier panel about Europeans and local content requirements. Those have been in place.

Our analysis suggests that they are of marginal significance. Essentially, the market for wind energy was created in Denmark. All the industry was therefore created, and they exported. As soon as Germany ramped up its market, its companies started manufacturing. Then again in Spain.

The reason why this has been more challenging in the United States is because the United States uniquely amongst those countries has yet to put in place a consistent long-term regime for the support of those technologies. As soon as you do, necessarily, those technologies will be manufactured here.

Wind turbines are 100 meter high towers and very, very long blades. It's actually relatively hard to move those around. If you know that you've got a long-term market, it makes much more sense to build a factory. If you don't know, then you will export from somewhere else.

So that is a critically important issue. There are millions and millions of Americans out of work. Every American out of work is a human tragedy, but it is also a broader tragedy for the world as a whole that these productive members of society are not having their skills harnessed for this important technology revolution.

I wanted to touch just briefly on the issue of border adjustments that you raised. I think it's been widely accepted that Congress is very likely to include some variant of that kind of provision in any likely climate bill.

Under certain conditions, I think that that may be justified. There are obviously concerns about leakage of manufacturing in critical sectors. There are a couple of notes of caution that should be sounded.

First of all, in Europe, where I worked for many years, there has been a long discussion about border adjustments, and the target in the crosshairs there is the United States. The U.S. has yet to apply a carbon price although Europeans have been looking at 40 bucks a ton, and what's sauce for the goose is sauce for the gander. So one of the things that we need to bear in mind in throwing that option out there is that it cuts both ways.

Secondly, timing, and I'm not a WTO lawyer, and if life teaches us one thing, is that a layman should not offer legal advice. But there are a number of WTO issues that are raised, particularly, as other countries are putting commitments on the table around climate, that they will argue that those are equivalent in various ways, and we need to be careful that we're not starting what is after all for the United States a first step in engaging seriously on climate policy, starting by upping the ante on the antagonism.

So I think that argues for some presidential discretion. It argues for some timing questions, but nevertheless, I think it is going to be part of the armory that the United States brings to that discussion.

MS. HSU: Just to add to those comments, at Copenhagen, this idea of a border tax adjustment was brought up to the Chinese delegation, and they did react very negatively to the idea, and they said this is a violation of WTO rules, and they said that if the United States were to enact some sort of border adjustment, we heard Chinese officials say they would be very opposed to it.

And then also I think that some analysis that Rob and my former colleagues at WRI did, looking at where the emissions, which sectors the emissions are coming from in China, is also a very useful and interesting analysis when Congress is considering how effective the border tax adjustment would be in influencing climate policy in China.

If you look at all the heavy industrial sectors in China, such as cement, iron and steel, oil and gas, a lot of these industries are being consumed or a lot of these products are being consumed domestically. And that's the majority of or that represents a huge portion of China's emissions.

For example, the Chinese cement sector is responsible for over half of CO_2 emissions in China. So placing a border tax adjustment that would tax cement wouldn't really do that much because the emissions would still occur, and cement would be produced regardless for domestic infrastructure and construction. So that was one point, I think, in Rob's analysis in the Leveling the Carbon Playing Field (publication), that really resonated.

Two years ago, when I was still working at WRI, I collaborated with a Low Carbon Energy Research Institute at Tsinghua University, and this is also an issue that they're looking very closely into. They're trying to get a better hold of where the emissions are coming from in the different sectors, and also the life cycle embedded carbon within many of their products.

So I think this is another area also where U.S. researchers could work with China to get a better handle of where the emissions are coming from in terms of the sectors, and whether or not a border tax adjustment, as Rob mentioned, would really be politically the way to go.

HEARING CO-CHAIR SHEA: Thank you.

Commissioner Fiedler.

COMMISSIONER FIEDLER: Dr. Economy, your written testimony gets into the question of China straddling the fence between being a developing nation and a global power. I know this is slightly unfair, but so when do you think they finally make a decision? When do you think they just have to declare themselves effectively or behave themselves like a global power?

DR. ECONOMY: I think there's a pretty serious debate right now within the Chinese government about how soon China should grab the brass ring of global leadership or at least sit alongside the United States in that regard.

China had the saying, "China can best help the world by helping itself"--which reflected the sense that China should maintain a low profile—and continue to grow its economy, a Deng Xiaoping sort of view of where China should be.

This remains the predominant view within China, but there are younger people, certainly within the world of finance and banking, that believe that China has arrived and is ready to step up to the plate. They want to assert China's role as a global power.

In any respect where China would feel that somehow its development would be compromised, it will be difficult to bring them along, and China still has strong concerns about sovereignty.

As a result, the United States is going to continue to pull and tug with China, but I think it's an internal debate as well as the pressure coming from the international community.

COMMISSIONER FIEDLER: Let me address your comment about their conduct in negotiations in Copenhagen, and less about Copenhagen but your observation that they sent their Premier there with no room to negotiate. We negotiate with them--now, admittedly, this is a multilateral negotiation—you've got to really juggle this one--as opposed to our negotiations with them on Iran, on North Korea.

So is this a unique multilateral international problem? Or is it an international negotiation problem inherent in the system, as you alluded to, I think, at the end, that it was a systemic problem? And if it's a systemic problem, seems we're going to have to cope with it for quite some time.

DR. ECONOMY: I think there's virtually no strictly U.S.-China bilateral issue in some ways. If you look at any issue that the United States has raised with China, whether you're talking about Iran or you're talking about North Korea--

COMMISSIONER FIEDLER: They're smaller, smaller multilateral.

DR. ECONOMY: They're smaller multilateral--

COMMISSIONER FIEDLER: That's what I mean.

DR. ECONOMY: --groupings, but they're still multilateral.

COMMISSIONER FIEDLER: Yes.

DR. ECONOMY: One of the things that we should learn, not only from Copenhagen, but also from other negotiations, is that it pays to think about who outside the United States or the EU or Japan, traditional powers, can be brought into negotiations to help bring China along?

In the case of the climate change negotiations, it might have been developing countries. In the case of Iran, it might be Saudi Arabia, and others.   COMMISSIONER FIEDLER: You were addressing a different issue.

DR. ECONOMY: Okay.

COMMISSIONER FIEDLER: Basically, the issue was they sent their negotiators there without any independent authority to make any decisions.

DR. ECONOMY: Ah.

COMMISSIONER FIEDLER: You said they offered everything--

DR. ECONOMY: Up front.

COMMISSIONER FIEDLER: --straight up off onto the table, and there was no movement.

DR. ECONOMY: Right.

COMMISSIONER FIEDLER: Now, everybody goes to negotiations representing their government and must report back to its government and ask for instructions. Here you would have to report back to the government and ask for instruction, and they'd have to commit the Politburo to a meeting, and decide where to go is where--

DR. ECONOMY: Right.

COMMISSIONER FIEDLER: --is what you were referring to, I think--

DR. ECONOMY: Okay.

COMMISSIONER FIEDLER: --when you said systemic problem.

DR. ECONOMY: I understand what you're asking now. In the case of North Korea and Iran, these are ongoing negotiations that are focused on a very distinct set of issues, and everybody is at the table almost all the time because they are smaller. You have Germany and others talking about Iran with the United States, and with China. It's not really the same kind of "here we are at this last moment," and no country is quite sure what is the others are bringing to the table.

Contrarily, everybody thinks they know what's coming to the table, but nobody quite knows where they have room to negotiate. I think in the Iranian case, there's a lot more back and forth that's going on among this small group all along the space of the negotiation. It's a different kind of negotiation.

COMMISSIONER FIEDLER: One last final characterization of this. I'm searching for an understanding. Therefore, is their multilateral negotiation like Copenhagen unsophisticated or immature?

DR. ECONOMY: I don't know that I'd characterize it that way.

COMMISSIONER FIEDLER: She's whispering in my ear. We're talking--or just simply unprepared?

DR. ECONOMY: As Ms. Hsu said, they put everything up front and that's where they ended up, and what surprised them was the extent to which they were blamed for Copenhagen going awry. Otherwise, we probably wouldn't be having this discussion in the same way.

I don't want to characterize their negotiation strategy as immature or unsophisticated. It's different. It's not flexible and therefore problematic, but it's their strategy.

MR. BRADLEY: Could I add a small thought on this?

COMMISSIONER FIEDLER: I've overdone my time.

VICE CHAIR BARTHOLOMEW: You have.

HEARING CO-CHAIR SHEA: Sure, if you want something to add, Mr. Bradley.

MR. BRADLEY: Thank you.

Just a thought in addition to Liz's very thoughtful analysis. The big problem here I think was not about China, it was not about the U.S.

It was that for the first time heads of state being brought into this process, and they were brought in incompetently.

In all of the other processes and in any decently managed diplomatic process, technocrats should be beavering away for months and months, and they should present a set of clear understandable options to heads of state. Heads of state were just outraged. They arrived in Copenhagen with essentially a blank sheet of paper, and their technocrats said, yes, we got nothing.

And that was the problem. Some countries found that more difficult than others, and the United States, I would venture to suggest, had a head of state that was particularly intellectually sophisticated and versatile in that regard. A lot of countries had real problems with that.

Many heads of state said I don't come here to negotiate a technical issue. It's complicated. It's too political for the technocrats and it's too technical for the politicians, and that's the real reason for the explosion we saw there.

The take-away from that is that that doesn't have to happen again. So, there are some important lessons there about how you engage higher political authority within those countries, but that I think was the underlying cause of the blowup.

HEARING CO-CHAIR SHEA: Thank you.

Vice Chair Bartholomew.

VICE CHAIR BARTHOLOMEW: Thanks very much, and thank you for all of our witnesses. I particularly want to single out Ms. Hsu because I'm always very pleased to see new and younger voices--no offense to some of the older voices. We love your expertise. We have the older voices up here too, but I'm just always pleased to see people engaging in the process. So thank you very much for taking the time. You're clearly an early adopter.

If you have that iPad up and running—today is Thursday. You picked it up on Saturday?

MS. HSU: I got it on Saturday, yes.

VICE CHAIR BARTHOLOMEW: Did you stand in line?

MS. HSU: No, there was no line actually.

VICE CHAIR BARTHOLOMEW: I'd like to, though, follow up on this issue of negotiating strategy. I bristled actually at the words that Jeff offered as options, but I want to put it in the context, first. Dr. Economy, when we talk about multilateralizing any of these issues, I think that the United States is often--I'm going to use the word "naive"--in confronting the reality that the Chinese come into this with their own interests in mind. We sense a more global responsibility, and clearly the Chinese are struggling to find their place in the world. They're struggling with that, too, but in a different place.

So they've got Iranian oil interests. They've got their own things going on. What I wonder about is post-Copenhagen. We have certainly seen over the course of the past year increased Chinese assertiveness in the world about the rightness of their own positions, particularly in terms of the global financial crisis and other issues.

When we were in China last year, I think we were all struck by the stridency with which the Chinese addressed a number of issues. You've heard about Tibet. You've heard about Taiwan from them repeatedly. But really stridency and a more digging in on their positions rather than trying to address some of the global concerns about what's going on.

Do we have evidence that what they have taken away from Copenhagen is the lessons that we think are the lessons from Copenhagen. Orr why do we believe when they have a system that has done things a particular way, through technocrats, for example, why do we believe that they would think that that's not a way to continue doing things, and that the rest of the people need to accommodate, and what goes along with that is shaping the perception of what happened after Copenhagen? This is for any of you.

MR. BRADLEY: I'm happy to take a first shot at that. I don't think you should believe anything of the sort. I don't think American negotiators are naive about this in the slightest. I actually happen to think you have brilliant negotiators, certainly in this process, who I think were given a very light hand and dealt it extraordinarily well.

The United States and China both operate in that process on the basis of national interests, as should be expected. And both, in fact, came to the table in that process not really negotiating a whole lot. Both the U.S. delegation was absolutely clear right throughout the year. They said we will put on the table what Congress tells us we can put on the table. And nice to talk to you, nice to meet you all, but you don't get to negotiate our number. Congress will negotiate our number, and we will report back to you on what it is.

And China came in exactly the same way. They said we've had a national process; we've had a national dialogue. Here's our target, and I think they thought that was going to be a much more pleasant process than they actually had in Copenhagen.

But I think it's fair to say that most of the major countries, with a couple of exceptions, the Europeans and Australians came with essentially two numbers and said you can negotiate us from one to the other, but most countries came with fairly clear ideas of what their offer was.

Now that doesn't mean that the international interaction doesn't matter. It matters over longer-time scales. It's not going to be negotiated over two weeks. But countries are going to watch what each other are doing over several years, and I think that will affect profoundly what they're prepared to do, and I think that will affect China and the U.S. both.

But I think that is not fundamentally just a characterization of the Chinese negotiating stance. I think it goes for the majority of countries.

As regards their growing assertiveness, one of the reasons why that particular process was so fascinating is that it is a case study of a country very much in transition on this. The U.S. is getting what we asked for. Countries sought to make China behave more like a world power around the financial crisis because its support was very much needed. And that is something I think that they're wrestling with, and they actually find uncomfortable, but that they're in the process of making that transition.

VICE CHAIR BARTHOLOMEW: I just want to add one clarification. In terms of negotiation strategy, I think that makes sense, what you said, but if we then get to the issue of negotiating styles, the process itself, is there evidence that the Chinese believe, that they're willing to empower the people who are at any of these tables to make decisions? And if not, what happens next?

MR. BRADLEY: My guess is that they will empower the individuals at those processes to make decisions around many of the things that the U.S. empowers the administration to make decisions about, i.e., not setting the target, not necessarily having the purse strings, but they will negotiate around the structure of verification and reporting mechanisms, around the processes by which countries set spending priorities, those kinds of things, and that I think the Chinese delegation will tend to have those kinds of authorities.

As I say, I don't think many countries are empowering their negotiators to negotiate away big things, and in fact I think that's actually an indicator of how seriously it's being taken. You don't just let your environment minister now run around making big promises because I think countries are more likely to think that that will land them with something they have to deliver.

DR. ECONOMY: I'll add that I think it is a slightly more profound issue within China, though, and a frequent complaint or concern within the United Nations has always been, very traditionally been, that the Chinese end up holding things up because they have to call back to Beijing to find out what are my instructions. We hadn't anticipated this new wrinkle into this particular issue; how do I deal with that? I don't have the authority to make that decision.

There probably is something, if not unique to China, that other countries have recognized can be a challenge in negotiations with China.

I would guess that as China becomes more confident, truly confident and secure in their role, that they will begin to give more authority to some of their players. But this has been a very traditional problem for the Chinese, at least within the United Nations.

HEARING CO-CHAIR SHEA: Thank you.

Commissioner Mulloy.

COMMISSIONER MULLOY: Thank you, Mr. Chairman.

I see two different issues that are kind of going on in today's hearing. The first is the effort to deal with international environmental global warming issues, and on those I'm very sympathetic that every effort to work with the Chinese. When I was a young man, I worked for Chris Herter, Jr., at the State Department and was involved in the first U.N. Conference on the Human Environment and I think these areas are very serious matters, and I think we have to approach them on a multilateral basis.

Now, I also see another thing going on in this hearing. China has an industrial policy. Part of China's industrial policy is to become the leader in green technologies, and they have certain policies in place, as we went through in the other panel, that incentivize U.S. companies to move operations from here to there, produce there, at the expense of people here and jobs here and our own people. And on that I think we have to figure out how we defend our interests.

Then I want to get into a question for Ms. Economy. In your testimony, on page five, you say "Chinese investment funds"--who does that mean--"are searching for new energy opportunities in the United States." What do you mean "Chinese investment funds"?

DR. ECONOMY: For example, the Chinese Investment Corporation and the State Administration of Foreign Exchange. I think there are a number of Chinese investment funds that are looking to move out of buying U.S. debt.

COMMISSIONER MULLOY: Yes.

DR. ECONOMY: And thinking what they can explore here.

COMMISSIONER MULLOY: Yes, exactly. So that's what I thought. What we have to understand in thinking about those Chinese investment funds--these are state-owned funds, state-controlled vehicles. So if we're saying, you, state-owned vehicle, can buy up clean technology companies in the United States, and we have to think very carefully about whether we really want that because these U.S. companies might be developing new technologies that can help the leadership of the United States in these, and we're going to hand over ownership or significant ownership interest to Chinese government entities.

When we're looking at an American corporation investing

somewhere, that's a different thing than if you're looking for a Chinese investment vehicle owned by the Chinese government investing here. Do you see a difference in that? Is that something that we should think carefully as a nation in what we're doing?

DR. ECONOMY: We have thought carefully about it. We have the Committee on Foreign Investment in the Unites States review process to determine whether or not there are industries that are core to our national security interests. We should use that process as we have in the past.

If we're looking to further develop our energy sector, however, we should welcome Chinese investment. Again, if there are key issues of technology that are core to our national security, then not. Otherwise, we believe in a free and open trading system, and whether it's a state-owned company in China should not be a reason to refuse investment. Investment capital from China is likely to come through major large-scale companies or a state-owned investment firm in China.

COMMISSIONER MULLOY: Mr. Bradley.

MR. BRADLEY: These are immensely important issues. Chinese industrial policy is significant, but by far the most important reason why companies move activities to China is to access the Chinese market. If we, the Chinese are creating a more consistent, more predictable market for these clean technologies than we are currently in the United States, and accordingly companies move there.

If we create that market in the United States, we will have the jobs in the United States. There are plenty of wrinkles to industrial policy, but the underlying piece is that simple: no market; no jobs.

While we should, and I'll come to this in a second, be vigilant about some of these activist government policies that you mention, we shouldn't lose sight of the fact that those are, to some extent, wrinkles on the bigger picture, which is about creating a market for these clean technologies in which American innovation ought to be completely dominating. This is what America is great at.

Do we want the energy business to be a commoditized old-school thing? Do we really think that's America's comparative advantage? Or does America win when it's about innovation, when it's about new inventions, when it's about engineering and so forth? So I really want to lay that out as the bigger picture.

As Liz said, there are responses to specific concerns. Congress' response to the Unocal purchase three or four years ago now is another example of where in a given instance Congress stepped in and said we feel there's a national interest question here at stake, and so those options are there.

If we think that China is actually undertaking genuinely

protectionist activities, the reason why we brought them into the WTO is precisely to try and create a legal structure in which they can be encouraged to play by the rule set. Those tools are all available if we think that there are really discriminatory things there.

As far as Chinese investment funds go, the Chinese have been saving a lot of money, and they need to invest it somewhere. They can invest it somewhere else, but I think, as Liz says, in general, we should welcome the fact that they invested in the U.S. I think fundamentally changing that dynamic takes us into a discussion of U.S. savings rates, which is probably beyond the scope of this particular discussion.

MS. HSU: Just briefly, I think that this is a perfect example, and it makes the argument for more collaboration between the U.S. and China on these technologies. As Rob mentioned, the U.S. is very good at innovation, and that's where the U.S. should be specializing in these partnerships, but the Chinese are also very good at mass production. So I think that the two together could really push the market.

Also, another untapped market is the Chinese domestic market for renewable technologies. Most of the market currently is export-driven in China so they manufacture a lot of solar PV and wind technology, but it goes to other places. And so you have a lot of huge Chinese companies within China who aren't taking advantage of a lot of these markets. I think that's another area where you could see U.S. helping to build Chinese domestic markets. So just those three points.

COMMISSIONER MULLOY: Do you mind if I just make one comment? The Congress did not block CNOOC from buying Unocal. There was concern in the House of Representatives, and then the government-owned corporation of China, CNOOC, decided that it would not pursue the transaction. There was no blockage by the United States.

HEARING CO-CHAIR SHEA: All right. Thank you.

Commissioner Reinsch.

HEARING CO-CHAIR REINSCH: Thank you.

First, I want to commend the staff, Ms. Levkowitz, in particular, and the hearing co-chairs for coming up with such good witnesses, not just on this panel, but on the others. This has been very enlightening and interesting.

The good questions, particularly about Copenhagen, have already been asked and answered. I want to pursue the train of thought that Commissioner Mulloy began. Well, that he pursued in turn from something that Mr. Bradley said earlier, that the jobs are where the market is, which is an interesting thought, and I think there is some skepticism up here about whether that's going to turn out to be true in this case.

I want to pursue that a little bit. Pat kind of did that, and rather than tread over the same ground, let me bring it up in the context of what Ms. Hsu just said about innovation. That complementarity, if you will, has been observed before.

One of the questions that we wrestle with is the extent to which innovation capability and actual innovation is moving out of here and over to China, and that the relationship that you've described of manufacture, if you will, and inventor is evolving, and that the Chinese are rapidly turning the corner, particularly in this sector, to becoming innovators and designers of original technology rather than simply more efficient producers of technology that somebody else has invented.

To the extent that's true, I think it casts some doubt on the accuracy, Mr. Bradley, of what you are predicting is going to happen.

So perhaps all three of you could comment on the extent to which the center of innovation in this technology, solar, wind and elsewhere, is moving, and what the implications of that are for the accuracy of Mr. Bradley's hypothesis?

MR. BRADLEY: Thank you for that question.

I will be very happy to follow-up by sharing some written studies with the Commission. We've actually been engaged with the Peterson Institute in exploring precisely these issues.

I think there are a couple of dimensions. One is about comparative advantage, and the other is about just the fundamental nature of some of these markets. In terms of comparative advantage, China, like South Korea before it, like Japan before South Korea, like the Europeans before them, want to move into higher value-added parts of the value chain. Everybody aspires to do that.

Certainly they're making a lot of efforts in that regard. I think one shouldn't overestimate the state of play at the moment. There still remains a vast gap between the United States and other Western economies, on the one hand, and countries like China, on the other, and that the comparative advantage is very much there for the time being.

We only have to see the balance of value chains in things like IT to see that this is still an area in which the vast majority of the research and development of the real innovation parts of the chain still reside in the West, and in the United States in particular. I think that will persist for a long time to come.

The broader point, though, is that if we look at what it takes to make solar power, for instance, most of the value of that is not really exportable. Even the panels, which typically account for about 25 percent of the cost of a solar project, those are becoming increasingly commoditized and moving down the scale just like memory chips did, and now they're all manufactured elsewhere.

Most of it is either in R&D or it's marketing or it's systems installation or it's building integration. Those things don't move. Similarly, with wind power. All the evidence that we have is that every country that builds a market ends up with the manufacturing done mainly nearby. Where that market is small, where it's sporadic, where it's fragmented, it becomes less easy to do.

But while nobody should blithely make predictions about the future, I think there are strong reasons to believe that these are basically facts that will remain true, as we go forward, and that this is an enormous opportunity that the U.S. will be taking.

I do want to underscore just how unique the United States still is in some of these spaces. Over the last few years, I've been fairly regularly going over to Silicon Valley and meeting the hyper-caffeinated youngsters there who all want breakfast at 5 a.m.--damn them--

[Laughter.]

MR. BRADLEY: --and who are just brimming with ideas and innovation. It's a very exciting space. One of the great tragedies for the United States and for the world is that incredible ingenuity has yet to be properly harnessed for the clean energy revolution.

HEARING CO-CHAIR REINSCH: Ms. Hsu, do you have a comment or not?

MS. HSU: No.

HEARING CO-CHAIR REINSCH: You're going to play it safe. All right. Dr. Economy.

DR. ECONOMY: By and large, I agree with Mr. Bradley's comments. However, we can't be complacent. While I think we do have an overall innovation edge, it's far from clear to me. As we can see, China is beginning to claim its own space in some sectors, and we can't sit and rest on our laurels and think we have a 15 to 20 year head start, and there is no reason that the Chinese are ever going to get there.

China will get there, and we have to continue to think about the kinds of things that Mr. Bradley was talking about, namely, creating our own market. The right regulation and market incentives help to spur innovation.

I also wonder whether or not China isn't "game-changing" when it comes to the issue of siting manufacturing near the market, and whether or not China is a low-cost manufacturer with such incredible capacity and low labor costs, that it is changing the nature of the game. I mean the markets in Spain and Germany developed in advance of that in China, and China's just developing its market now.

Is it possible that with all of those low cost labor advantages and others there's a game-changing aspect to this in China, that we wouldn't see with Germany or Spain or some others? That's something we need to look at.

HEARING CO-CHAIR SHEA: Thank you.

I just have a quick last question, and it's back to Copenhagen. You made the point that the Chinese went into Copenhagen with a bottom line position with no flexibility whatsoever built into their negotiating stance.

I've read in a couple of places that Wen Jiabao was publicly criticized by some of his subordinates in public forums, that he was going off text, going off position. Have you heard that? Are those stories true?

And number two, if they are true, what did he agree to that was not part of the initial bottom line position?

MR. BRADLEY: I was not personally in the room. I have other accounts including published media accounts. To deal with your last question first--this was all about the verification question. And the United States came in really with two fundamental demands of China. One, you've got to step up for the first time and take a commitment; but, secondly, we need to have a verification regime.

There is no getting around the fact that is intensely uncomfortable territory for China. It's not been big on transparency. I think we can all agree on that as a starting point.

President Obama directly engaging with Wen Jiabao was really pushing this issue. How far can we go in trying to have language that says, listen, you have to report your data, but we don't have to just take it at face value; we have to check up on it. And Xie Zhenhua, who is the head climate negotiator, had been particularly reluctant to move on this issue. Wen Jiabao, on this telling of the story, was starting to negotiate.

Xie Zhenhua had a certain outburst in Chinese. Wen Jiabao turned to the translators and instructed them not to translate what he had just said, but I think this is illustrative of the (a) the difficulty of that issue for the Chinese, and the significance, therefore, of what the U.S. won, which I think is really important.

Secondly, of the difficulty and complexity of having the head of state come into that role and essentially have to negotiate around something where there is 20 years of baggage on that stuff. Every nuance, every word is loaded. I mean the English language is entirely bereft now of words that are uncontaminated by some kind of term of art meaning in the climate process, and I'm sure that the same is true for Chinese.

In fact, the Ministry of Foreign Affairs and the National Development Reform Commission have different translations of the word "verification," which imply different levels of stringency. So anyway, that, I think, is the context for the incident you're referring to. And the achievement on the verification language is, I think, a significant one.

HEARING CO-CHAIR SHEA: Okay.

DR. ECONOMY: Just a quick point of clarification. I thought the outburst was actually directed at President Obama, not at Premier Wen Jiabao.

HEARING CO-CHAIR SHEA: No, there was an outburst directed at President Obama according to the public reports I've read.

DR. ECONOMY: And that was by Xie Zhenhua.

HEARING CO-CHAIR SHEA: But I've also read in a public forum, public document what you--

MR. BRADLEY: The New York Times reported an outburst at Wen Jiabao.

HEARING CO-CHAIR SHEA: Yes.

MR. BRADLEY: I'm sure there was also an outburst at President Obama.

DR. ECONOMY: Yes.

HEARING CO-CHAIR SHEA: Thank you very much. I echo my colleagues' comments about the quality of the panel, and appreciate you sharing your expertise with us, and we will adjourn until 1:20, and we'll have our last and final panel for the day.

Thank you.

[Whereupon, at 12:37 p.m., the hearing recessed, to reconvene at 1:20 p.m., this same day.]

AFTERNOON SESSION

PANEL IV: U.S.-CHINA COOPERATION ON GREEN ENERGY

HEARING CO-CHAIR REINSCH: Welcome back, everybody. In our final panel today, we will examine U.S.-China cooperation on green energy and the implications of this cooperation for the United States.

We have three very distinguished witnesses with us. Mr. Dennis Bracy spearheads the U.S.-China Clean Energy Forum. He has led the U.S. team for the forum since the inception of the organization in 2007. Mr. Bracy also chairs the Washington State China Relations Council.

Over the past 20 years, he has served as a key advisor to Senators, governors, and Members of Congress, and is considered a leading strategist on political and public affairs issues.

Also with us today is Mr. L. Cartan Sumner, Jr., Vice President of International Government Relations with Peabody Energy in St. Louis.

In this role, he is responsible for working with governments to create a friendly policy framework for the greater use of coal to meet growing energy needs and support Peabody's global expansion.

Mr. Sumner previously served as Director of Corporate Development with Peabody from 2001-2007. Prior to joining Peabody Energy, Mr. Sumner was Director of Corporate Development with RPM, Inc., a specialty chemical holding company based near Cleveland, Ohio.

Our final witness on this panel is Mr. Albert Tramposch, Deputy Executive Director at the American Intellectual Property Law Association. A patent attorney with a background in environmental sciences, Albert Tramposch is a former Director of Industrial Property Law at the World Intellectual Property Organization in Geneva.

In addition to his work there, he has practiced intellectual property law in the United States and internationally and has taught at several U.S. law schools, as well as having served as a member of the U.S. Patent and Trademark Office Policy Advisory Committee.

Thank you, all three of you, for joining us. We'll proceed in the order in which I introduced you. Your full written statements, will be placed in the record, and we'll ask you to limit your oral remarks to seven minutes each.

Mr. Bracy.

STATEMENT OF MR. DENNIS BRACY
CHIEF EXECUTIVE OFFICER, U.S.-CHINA CLEAN ENERGY
FORUM, SEATTLE, WASHINGTON

MR. BRACY: Thank you, Chairman Reinsch, and members of the Commission.

I will spare you the full reading of my remarks. A guy I used to work for, Mo Udall, who was chairman of the Interior Committee, used to say everything that can be said on the subject has been said, but not everyone has said it, and I will now fall into that trap.

I will tell you a little bit about why we got started and how, and how we've approached things, and perhaps what we've learned along the way, and then I'd be delighted to have the kind of spirited interchange I've seen earlier today. The questions and the comments have been terrific. You've heard a lot of smart people so I won't cover the same territory. The numbers are pretty well understood.

We started--a friend, Maria Cantwell, Senator from Washington, went to China three-and-a- half years ago, and gave a speech to a thousand women entrepreneurs, and said we're the largest energy users in the world, almost 50 percent of the whole deal. We've got a choice. We can go down one road of competing against each other endlessly for scarce resources with all the terrible things that means for the environment, the economy, and geopolitical security.

Or we can put a stake in the ground and decide to mount a moon-shot-level cooperative program on clean energy and efficiency. She then met with Zhang Guobao, who is still the strongman. He's the Vice Chairman of the NDRC and the Director of the National Energy Administration, and effectively the leader of the new National Energy Commission, which Wen Jiabao heads, with 23 members.

And they hit it off, and she said we need some summits. We need to get a dialogue going here. And then we got to do the work. So the NDRC, the National Development Reform Commission, was named as the China lead. We were lucky enough to be able to recruit some very smart and wise people--Stan Barer, who actually opened U.S. trade in 1979 with the arrival of the Liu Lin Hai into the port of Seattle; Carla Hills; Mickey Kantor; Bill Brock; Norm Mineta, a bipartisan group of people who had great experience and wisdom--to share with us about how to go at it.

We did two things that I think bear some note. One is that we did not attack the overall issue of climate change. We went strictly for clean energy and efficiency, which is perhaps 70 percent of climate change, but we have avoided some of the theological issues of who's responsible for what and who pays and so on. Those are tough, and those are important.

But we concentrated on clean energy and efficiency because we see absolute common interests. We're really in the same boat. As the largest energy users and coal users and automobile markets and infrastructure developers, we're very much in the same position. We both import about 60 percent of our oil, and believe me, China is just as scared about that as we are.

So we started from that premise, and then we further said any recommendations we make to our governments will only be made if we 100 percent agree. Every word. So there is no minority report from China, no minority report from the U.S.

And we labored. We put together hundreds of wonderful experts from companies, National Laboratories, universities, on both sides, and we worked and developed eight initiatives, and they range from clean cars to advanced coal to efficiency, but one area that leapt out, and something I'd like to concentrate on because I know you've delved into this a bit, is that we, U.S. and China, have signed 45 cooperative agreements since 1979. We're really good at the signing agreements thing.

Ever since Secretary Schlesinger led that first group, we've been signing well-intentioned agreements that move in the right direction, but what we haven't really done effectively is get at the barriers, get at the policy barriers, get at the business barriers, because that's the only way we're going to get the full benefits of commerce and the widest deployment of these technologies in both our countries.

Those are IP issues, which I'm sure you'll hear about. Those are financing issues. Those are trade and tariff, and export control issues. So we spent some time working on that, and I would say in the early days, it was a little bit foreign territory for the NDRC. They're very powerful; they're very smart. They know a lot about energy, but export controls and financing and issues like that were not in their sweet spot.

But after two years, we came to some agreements, and I'd be happy to forward some fairly detailed language that we agreed on that I think offers the blueprint, not only for project by project cooperation, which is important, but more systemic cooperation, to benefit both sides and ultimately the world.

And that included things like creating a new organization, kind of an experiment, concentrating on clean energy to provide IP insurance. Any U.S. or Chinese company could sign up for this, pay a premium, and it would be backed by the full faith and credit of both governments. Those premiums would actually fund an enforcement arm, and I think it would give the markets some confidence that's not there now. It would be a registry, like ASCAP is for music rights, for intellectual property, and we say let's limit it to clean energy because we can't solve world hunger in one bite here.

We need to do something manageable. There are other models that we're looking at that are intriguing in Hong Kong. You see where Hong Kong can be an IP lockbox under the rule of law of Hong Kong, and the manufacturing can occur across the border in Shenzhen. Chongqing is providing IP insurance in order to attract business. Singapore outside China does the same thing.

We see movement in this area. We think patent pools might be a good way to build on our joint Clean Energy Research Center. We're going to create joint IP, right? Well, why don't we try to also invent systems that will protect both sides? Because when I go around China, and I meet with the BYDs and the ENNs and the Suntechs, and the GCLs of the world, and I go through their slide show, slide two inevitably is here are our patents; here is our intellectual property. And we're seeing a change. So I think that creativity can go a long, long way.

Finally, a comment, and I'll turn it over to my colleagues here, and I suspect I take a different point of view than some who have testified today. We believe that bilateral is the way to go to begin this multilateral process. I think getting 192 countries to agree on anything is a very, very tough proposition, but when the U.S. and China together represent nearly 50 percent of the total, I think there's--and we found great resonance within this clean energy and efficiency arena, and I think we've always thought it's possible to do a bilateral, and from a bilateral we can go outward and build the multilateral through APEC, for example, and then take it to the world.

It's not a popular strategy, but I think Copenhagen showed that maybe the other way isn't the most effective way.

So with that, I turn it back to the chair.

[The statement follows:]

Prepared Statement of Mr. Dennis Bracy, Chief Executive Officer, U.S.-China Clean Energy Forum, Seattle, Washington

My goal today is to share perspectives we've gained from more than three years of working with Chinese leaders to forge a pragmatic and effective cooperative clean energy program between the world's two largest energy users.

I'd also like to offer some comments on the Administration's efforts to promote joint research and eliminate trade and policy barriers. More on that later.

WHERE WE ARE

To judge by the headlines, over the past few years we've gone from "China is adding two new, dirty coal plants a week and doesn't care about the environment," to "China is doing laps around the US and is going to steal our jobs and dominate the clean energy sector for years to come."

The truth, I believe, is much more nuanced than those headlines would indicate. If we want to understand how we to transform to a clean energy economy, we need to dig beneath the headlines and look at what's really happening on the ground.

That's why this is a perfect time for this commission, and for our country as a whole, to examine the risks, understand the opportunities, and implement a plan of action that will benefit both our countries. I applaud the commission for diving into this important issue.

US-CHINA COOPERATION

But first, a bit of background on the US-China Clean Energy Forum.

In November of 2006, Senator Maria Cantwell gave an important speech to more than 1,000 women business leaders in Beijing.

In that speech, Senator Cantwell said "The US and China are the largest energy users in the world, and we consume nearly half the energy on the planet. We've hit a "Y" in the road. In coming decades, we can either compete with each other for resources all over the world, with all the terrible things that means for the environment, our economies and geopolitical security; or, we can put a stake in the ground and join together to mount a moon-shot-level program on clean energy and efficiency."

Senator Cantwell's speech struck a chord and was widely covered in Chinese media. Later, she met with vice chairman Zhang Guobao of the National Development and Reform Commission—China's top energy leader—and they agreed to work together to organize a process for increasing cooperation—and commerce—in clean energy and efficiency.

Minister Zhang's staff from the National Development and Reform Commission took the lead on the Chinese side.

Back in the US, we recruited a bipartisan group of leaders who have deep experience with China and with trade: founding co-chair Stan Barer; former US Trade Representatives Mickey Kantor, Carla Hills and Bill Brock, former cabinet secretary, Congressman and Mayor Norm Mineta; Sharon Nelson, chair of the board of Consumers Union; Sue Tierney, chair of the Energy Foundation and former Ambassador to China Stapleton Roy.

With their guidance and the support of hundreds of expert volunteers and nearly three dozen supporting sponsors—organizations like GE, Boeing, Energy Foundation, Honeywell, McKinsey, Applied Materials, Garvey Schubert Barer law firm, Itron, PriceWaterhouseCoopers, Consolidated Edison of New York, Puget Sound Energy, L&L Energy, Stark Investments, The Port of Seattle, PG&E, Better Place, Sapphire Energy, Hill & Knowlton, University of Washington, US-China Business Council, Amcham-Shanghai, Washington State University, Battelle, Washington State China Relations Council, the Woodrow Wilson International Center for Scholars, Avatar Studios, The Prosser Group and many more, we've been working to turn the vision of enhanced cooperation and increased commerce into a practical roadmap for both our countries.

EIGHT INITIATIVES FOR CLEAN ENERGY COOPERATION

We decided early on to concentrate on clean energy and efficiency, not the broader issue of climate change, so we could concentrate on common interests, rather than debating historic roles and issues of fairness. In clean energy and efficiency, our common interests are clear and well understood by both sides. China and the US are:

- The largest energy users and emitters of greenhouse gases
- The largest importers of petroleum and similarly vulnerable to supply shocks
- The world's largest automobile markets
- The largest electric grid and the biggest investors in energy infrastructure

We also decided the only recommendations we would make to our governments would be those in which we had absolute agreement from both sides. Over the course of three years, through numerous expert working group meetings in China and the US, we developed a joint set of eight recommendations:

1. *Establish a joint clean energy center* to collaborate on research and development projects, train energy efficiency experts and create a training program for lenders.

2. *Share knowledge and technologies needed to create Smart Grids* (including transmission and distribution networks) to increase efficiency and facilitate integration of variable resources such as wind and solar power.

3. Establish a coordinated program to *accelerate development of advanced coal projects*, including carbon capture and sequestration.

4. *Increase efficiency and lower manufacturing costs of solar* photovoltaic and solar hot water systems to make them competitive with traditional thermal resources. Set ambitious goals for deployment of renewable by 2020 in each country.

5. *Power the rollout of hybrid and pure electric motor vehicles* by aggressively building infrastructure for recharging, conducting joint research and development of battery technology and developing standards that will maximize trade and job creation.

6.   Develop bio-energy fuels and *sustainable transportation technologies for the aviation and maritime industries*, which are not able to rely only on batteries for power.

7.   *Utilize policy tools to eliminate barriers* such as import tariffs and export controls. Accelerate clean energy adoption by creating a sustainable financing system and establish a joint entity to protect intellectual property.

8.   Create *Strategic Energy Zones (SEZs)* to facilitate innovation in applying new policies, rate structures and tax incentives, etc. so that it will be easier to implement other priorities in the joint clean energy program.

These initiatives are ambitious, but achievable. They represent a healthy down payment on the "moon shot" cooperative effort that was our original call to action.

We are pleased to note that the concepts embodied in six of these initiatives were incorporated into the agreements signed by Presidents Obama and Hu in November. We are very supportive of the efforts of our government is taking to implement these agreements, and we are working to focus the efforts of the private sector to support the government-to-government initiatives.

REMOVING BARRIERS IS KEY TO LONG-TERM PROGRESS

But the work can't stop there. Despite our well-recognized common interests in accelerating deployment of clean energy technologies and creating jobs by increasing trade, a number of policy barriers prevent common interests and good intentions from being translated into the kind of wholesale action both countries need. In the past 30 years, the US and China have signed more than 45 cooperative energy agreements. All of them well-intentioned, but none of which has led to the kind of transformation we both need.

That's why, in initiative number seven, we focused on trade and policy barriers. Key recommendations include:

> • Minimizing or eliminating tariffs and non-tariff barriers on clean energy goods and services. Both the US and China currently impose import tariffs on a wide variety of clean energy technologies. China is now the largest exporter of many clean energy technologies and would benefit from the lowering or removal of tariffs.

> • Eliminating or greatly simplifying export controls for clean energy technology, software and services. A substantial barrier in perception and practice is the current US system of export controls which substantially delays and deters efforts for joint research and development of new technologies between the US and other nations. The combination of license requirements, dual use analyses, end user requirements and non-eligible trader lists served important national security needs in the past but now deter joint efforts to develop and implement multi-country use of best efforts to reduce carbon emissions. As Secretary Locke has pointed out, we can protect our legitimate national interests and still simplify the export process, so we encourage the widest possible deployment of clean energy technologies.

> • Instituting a joint intellectual property protection program with insurance jointly
> written by US and Chinese entities (for example by the US Export-Import Bank or similar

government program and by People's Insurance Company of China), with the full faith and credit of each government standing behind the policies. This would strengthen property rights on both sides and greatly increase confidence when transferring new technology or undertaking joint research. It would also encourage strong enforcement of laws against infringement of intellectual property rights.

• Instituting ongoing and sustainable financing mechanisms for clean energy, including direct financing, loans and loan guarantees that are appropriate for each country's situation.

• Sharing best practices on innovative energy rate structures to help manage demand and on incentives to accelerate clean energy deployment.

GETTING BEYOND STATISTICS
Co-chairs Reinsch and Shea, members of the Commission, when we began our efforts. the common wisdom was that China was not focused on clean energy and was in the process of building two 500-megawatt coal plants each week.

Three years later, I can tell you with absolute conviction that the landscape has changed dramatically.
In fact, I think it's fair to say that a new fever has taken over China in the past couple of years—a low-carbon fever. That fever is driven by the significant pollution issues that China continues to face, the knowledge that China cannot continue to fuel its growth with traditional forms of energy generation and a drive to reduce its dependence on other countries for energy.
The national statistics provide solid evidence for the new path that China has charted:

- China spent twice as much as any country on the world last year on renewable energy—more than $35 billion. They've done this by regulation and with a focused investment plan and a series of aggressive feed-in tariffs. Some of the projects are monumental in scale: 8-gigawatt wind farms in the western part of China and a 2-gigawatt solar photovoltaic project in Inner Mongolia—a solar farm larger in area than Manhattan. (This project, by the way, will be led by an American solar company—First Solar). Huaneng, one of the world's largest power producers, recently announced that 35% of its generation will come from renewable energy—by 2020. And overall, China has set a goal of getting 15% of its power from renewable sources by 2020.

- With the assistance of US national laboratories and non-profit organizations such as the Energy Foundation, China has greatly improved its building and appliance energy standards. They require automobiles to achieve 35 miles per gallon or higher, a standard which takes hold in the US in 2016. They instituted a clunker tax and gave generous tax rebates to stimulate the market for energy-efficient cars. They are moving aggressively to electric vehicles for fleets and already have public charging stations in several cities. They've already converted tens of millions of motor scooters to electricity.

- The commitment to mass transit and high-speed rail is evident in cities all over China. There are new subway lines, buses powered by electricity, 250 mile per hour rail lines. The new train from Beijing to Shanghai will cut transit time from 12 hours to four, and will be completed one year ahead of time. China has purchased hundreds of GE's energy-efficient locomotives.

- In Tianjin, Huaneng is nearing completion on a low-carbon coal gasification plant that will be among the most advanced in the world. They are working closely with several American companies to share information and accelerate progress in the areas of efficiency, cost, and adoption of carbon-lowering technology around the world.

- And China has become a leader in exporting clean technology to the rest of the world. This past year, they've become the world leader in solar and in wind exports. And they are well positioned to play a leading role in LED lights and advanced batteries.

The national statistics are notable, but it is the stories-behind-the-story that leave the strongest impressions:

- In Shaanxi Province, home of Xi'an and the terra cotta warriors, Governor Yuan Chunqing used a portion of his province's stimulus funds to provide 23,000 of the poorest families in Shaanxi, who have been living without access to electricity, with solar panels and batteries. Even better, with the assistance of Applied Materials, they provided training for the women of the village so they could earn money by starting micro-enterprises to maintain the new solar panels and batteries.

- In Yunnan province's capital city of Kunming, in southwest China, as you look out your hotel window, you can see solar hot water heaters on nearly every building. Costing only about $200, more than half the city's 5 million residents get their hot water from solar devices. In nearby Lijiang, the women of the village no longer have to spend eight months of every year gathering wood and dung for heat and cooking. Thanks to assistance from the Nature Conservancy, they have modern bio-digesters that create gas to heat their homes and cook their meals.

- Near Shanghai, the 20-mile long Donghai bridge connects Shanghai with Yangshan Island, which serves as an extension of the Port of Shanghai. Seeing that bridge, NDRC vice-chairman Zhang Guobao came up with an idea—and today there are 34 giant wind turbines alongside the bridge, which provide a total of 100 megawatts of power, enough for 170,000 families.

- All over China companies are building green businesses. Companies like BYD, Suntech and ENN are not only strong in China, but are becoming world-class competitors in solar, electric vehicles, grid storage, cleaner coal and algae-derived biofuels.

All in all, as one travels around China, it's hard not to conclude that some sort of low-carbon fever has taken hold. There are green buildings everywhere. Not only in the biggest international cities like Beijing, Shanghai and Shenzhen, but also in Changsha, Yangzhou, Jilin, Wuxi and Xi'an.
In Dalian, Shui On is developing a new city-within-a-city that will cut the carbon footprint by more than 60%, using existing technologies, with the capability to cut carbon further as new technologies become cost-effective.

Recently, at a conference in Shanghai, I met the Mayor of Liaoyuan, of Jilin province, who presented me with a list of eight initiatives for a low carbon economy, modeled on the eight initiatives developed by the Clean Energy Forum. The truth is I had never heard of Liaoyuan, whose economy was long based on coal, but somehow city officials heard about our joint efforts and created their own initiatives to transform their economy.

So, members of the Commission, let me say with some conviction that the low carbon movement in China is for real, and it is gaining momentum.
CHINA'S CHALLENGE

At this point, a reasonable person might ask: "So what's the problem? If China's leaders really get it, if they are truly investing so heavily in clean energy and efficiency, why has China become the world's largest emitter of greenhouse gases and why won't they agree to cap their emissions as part of an international agreement?"

As a regular visitor to China, I am constantly reminded of two megatrends that are fundamental to understanding China's energy situation:

- First, China is growing a middle class of hundreds of millions of people. People who suddenly find themselves with new prosperity. Prosperity that enables them to travel, to buy their first car, to meet friends at a restaurant, to install an air conditioner in their home, to buy a flat panel TV and a computer. It's happening in cities all over China, and even, to some extent, in rural China. More prosperity, more comfortable lifestyles, leads to increased energy use.

- Second, the largest migration in the history of the world is underway in China. Each year, twenty million people are moving from the countryside to the cities, seeking a better life and increased economic opportunity. Twenty million people every year means, over the next fifteen years, China has to build new infrastructure that is the equivalent of the United States: homes, schools, hospitals, stores, power plants, mass transportation, airports, roads, sewage plants and all the rest.

To put this in context, take a look at just one sector: automobiles. Today China has about 40 million light vehicles, compared with our 225 million. Last year, China leapfrogged the US to become the world's largest car market. By 2030, just 20 years from now, estimates are that China will have more than 350 million vehicles. That's a sobering number. If China adds that many vehicles using traditional internal combustion technologies, we're all in trouble.

Serious trouble. The impact on petroleum prices, air quality and greenhouse gas emissions would be enormous.

But if China takes a new approach, emphasizing mass transit and electric vehicles, they can meet that surge in demand without sending the price of petroleum through the roof, creating more pollution and overwhelming the world's efforts to contain greenhouse gas emissions. They can even make their electrical grid more efficient by storing otherwise wasted nighttime wind power in car batteries. I believe Chinese leaders understand this reality and are eager to cooperate with the US in helping to shape this transformation to an electric car future.

TIME IS THE ENEMY

The US and China have many common challenges, many common opportunities and some areas where we will inevitably compete. When it comes to energy, the watchword with China will be "coopetition."

As different as our countries are, we face one common challenge that trumps all others: time.

McKinsey & Company published a compelling analysis of what impact various technologies can have on reducing—or abating—the rise in greenhouse gases. They rank the potential abatement impact of key technologies and analyze whether, in today's world, deployment of those technologies makes economic sense.

Here's the scary part of their analysis: if we delay deployment of the cost-effective technologies by just five years, we lose 35-50% of our ability to capture that incremental carbon (essentially) forever, since greenhouse gases don't decay for 100 years or more.

So time is the common enemy and our imperative is to work as quickly as we can to implement the technologies that make sense today, while combining our brains and our budgets to create tomorrow's technologies and make them affordable.

A PRAGMATIC ROADMAP FOR COOPERATION

There's no doubt that there are significant differences between the US and China. It's no secret that we have and will continue to have disagreements over trade, currency, Taiwan and other issues. This Commission understands that landscape very well.

But when it comes to energy, China and the US are in the same boat. And even with the current tensions between our countries, we see no let up in China's willingness to cooperate on clean energy and efficiency.

Understanding our differences, but building on our mutual benefits, we can do more together, more quickly, than we can separately. It's that simple.

But a US-China bilateral agreement, if it is going to result in more than pilot projects and good intentions, needs to be built on a no-nonsense approach that includes putting the policies in place which will enable both countries to make the necessary investments, and leverage each other's strengths, so we can increase trade and create more jobs in both countries. That's a prescription for sustainable cooperation.

We need to continue and expand on the many joint projects underway by businesses, government agencies, national laboratories, NGOs and universities. We need to put our best teams forward to lead and provide sufficient funding for the US-China Clean Energy Research Center, which will be under the leadership of Secretary Stephen Chu and Assistant Secretary David Sandalow at the Department of Energy. By joining forces with Chinese researchers, for every dollar we invest, we can get many dollars in impact.

And we need to support Secretary Gary Locke's efforts to get at the barriers which have inhibited true, mutually-beneficial cooperation: trade and tariffs, intellectual property protection and financing. For our part, the US-China Clean Energy Forum will continue to tap into our network of energy, finance and legal experts so we can help both governments develop creative answers to these long-standing issues.

Co-chairs Reinsch and Shea, members of the Commission, thanks again for addressing this important issue and giving us the opportunity to share our perspective.

The time is right, the need is urgent and cooperation on clean energy simply makes good sense--for the United States, for China and for the world.

> HEARING CO-CHAIR REINSCH: Thank you.
> Mr. Sumner.

STATEMENT OF MR. L. CARTAN SUMNER, JR.
VICE PRESIDENT OF INTERNATIONAL GOVERNMENT
RELATIONS, PEABODY ENERGY, ST. LOUIS, MISSOURI

> MR. SUMNER: Thank you.
> Chairman Slane, Vice Chairman Bartholomew, Hearing Co-Chair Commissioner Reinsch, Hearing Co-Chair Commissioner Shea, and other distinguished Commissioners of the U.S.-China Economic and Security Review Commission, it is a great privilege as well as an honor for me to participate in this hearing.
> My name is Cartan Sumner, and I serve as Vice President of International Government Relations with Peabody Energy based in St. Louis, Missouri.
> Peabody Energy is the world's largest private sector coal

company. Our coal products fuel ten percent of all U.S. electricity and approximately two percent of the world's power. Peabody is among Fortune's Most Admired companies, and achieved more than 30 awards last year for corporate leadership, safety and environmental performance.

Peabody owns majority interests in 28 coal mining operations located in the United States and Australia. Last year, we sold coal to generating and industrial plants in 23 companies on six continents. We are expanding our global footprint in developing Asia with offices in Beijing, Jakarta and Ulaanbaatar, and a new trading hub in Singapore.

One of the issues, which you encouraged me to address, is the role of private companies in fostering U.S.-China cooperation on clean energy and environmental issues. Our view is that private companies can play a meaningful role.

In these remarks, my objective is to brief you on how Peabody is fostering such bilateral cooperation and the details of our partnerships in China. In the United States, Peabody has the largest production and reserve position in the Powder River Basin and in the Illinois Basin.

Our flagship operations are located in Wyoming where coal is extracted at enormous scale in modern and technologically advanced open pit or surface coal mining facilities. Our largest mine alone produces ten percent of America's annual coal production.

In Australia, Peabody is the fastest growing coal producer. Our Queensland and New South Wales production is sold primarily into the seaborne export market for steelmaking and electricity-generation in Japan, South Korea, India, and most recently China.

"When the mining is complete, we will leave the land in the condition that is equal to or better than we found it." This is a sentence from Peabody's mission statement and a core principle of our company. More than 25 awards were earned by Peabody in the past three years for land restoration, revegetation and good neighbor practices.

Safety is also core to Peabody's mission. Our company strives relentlessly to operate with not just zero injuries but zero incidents of any kind. The last three years have been our safest, and in 2009, the company earned 11 industry awards for excellence in safety and emergency preparedness.

Under the leadership of our Chairman and Chief Executive Officer Greg Boyce, the first measure of overall performance at Peabody is safety.

We believe that sustainability and safety are pertinent to this hearing because they are elements of how we seek to forge cooperation with China. In China, Peabody's aspiration is to be a long-term strategic energy partner. We seek to develop large-scale, modern and efficient open cut coal mining facilities similar to those we operate in the United States and Australia.

In doing so, we will bring to the Chinese market best-in-class environmental and land restoration practices while imbedding safety in every aspect of mining.

This is one role which a private company such as Peabody can play in fostering U.S.-China cooperation. Another is in the area of clean energy technology. Peabody is promoting the development of clean coal technologies that would reduce emissions from the use of coal.

We are doing so by participating in more than a dozen initiatives to advance technology in the United States, China and Australia.

One example is GreenGen. GreenGen is China's centerpiece climate initiative. It is a partnership between several major Chinese energy companies and Peabody to develop a commercial-scale, near-zero emissions, coal-fueled power plant with carbon capture and storage.

GreenGen is being developed in phases and construction is well underway. Peabody was invited to become the only non-Chinese equity partner in GreenGen. Our joint venture agreement was executed on November 17 last year in connection with President Obama's visit to China.

That same day, the GreenGen signing was recognized among the measures announced by President Obama and President Hu to strengthen bilateral cooperation on clean energy.

GreenGen represents a significant step between the U.S. and China in the area of energy and the environment. The partnership is establishing a model for international collaboration on these issues. We are very privileged to be involved.

Coal has been the world's fastest growing fuel each of the last six years. Over the next 20 years, global coal use is forecast to grow 53 percent. That's more than one-and-a-half times the combined growth rate of all other energy sources.

As the world continues to increase its use of coal, we must do more to achieve the world's climate policy goals and work towards near-zero emissions. The path for reduced emissions is technology and GreenGen provides a template.

Another channel for private companies to engage with China is the new U.S.-China Energy Cooperation Program. The ECP was established last October as a public-private partnership to leverage the resources of leading companies for advancing clean energy projects in China.

It is part of the implementing mechanism for the U.S.-China Ten Year Energy and Environment Cooperation Framework and is a platform to bring U.S. industry into the field of clean energy in China while promoting shared policy objectives of our two countries.

Peabody is both a founding corporate member of the ECP and a participant in the Executive Committee of the organization.

There is at least one other role which private companies can also play to foster U.S.-China cooperation on clean energy and the environment. That is through direct financial sponsorship of joint scientific research and development initiatives.

One such initiative is the Consortium for Clean Coal Utilization at Washington University in St. Louis. Washington University is one of America's foremost research institutions. With funding from Peabody and other industry partners, the university established the Consortium for Clean Coal Utilization, dedicated to addressing the scientific and technical challenges of ensuring that coal can be used in a clean and sustainable manner.

In the context of formal bilateral cooperation, efforts are underway to establish Washington University as a satellite research site of the U.S.-China Clean Energy Research Center, which was discussed this morning by Secretary Sandalow and which was launched last November.

Our hope is that combining one of America's finest universities with the support of local private industry, an international hub for clean coal technology development will emerge in America's heartland.

There is common ground among the leaders of the U.S. and China on the necessity of accelerating the development of clean energy technology. Peabody Energy is aggressively supporting this objective, which requires shared commitment on the part of government officials and industry from both nations.

Our hope is that in doing so, Peabody is playing a constructive role in broadening the extent of strategic cooperation between the United States and China.

I would again like to express my gratitude for the opportunity to testify before you today on this important topic. Thank you.

[The statement follows:][7]

HEARING CO-CHAIR REINSCH: Thank you.
Mr. Tramposch.

STATEMENT OF MR. ALBERT TRAMPOSCH DEPUTY EXECUTIVE DIRECTOR, AMERICAN INTELLECTUAL PROPERTY LAW ASSOCIATION, ARLINGTON, VIRGINIA

---

[7] Click here to read the prepared statement of Mr. L. Cartan Sumner, Jr.

MR. TRAMPOSCH: Thank you very much, Mr. Chairman, and members of the Commission.

I'd like to start, as we all have, by thanking you for the opportunity to join you and talk about what I think is one of the most important issues before us today.

The statements that I'll make today are on my own behalf only, not official positions of the Association, although I will refer at some points to positions that the Association has taken.

The American Intellectual Property Law Association is a national bar association of more than 16,000 members that are engaged in private and corporate practice, in government service, and in the academic community.

Our members represent both owners and users of intellectual property. And the Association has taken a very keen interest in the protection of green technology and, in particular, patents with respect to green technology.

We've recognized and supported the Obama Administration's efforts to promote green technology, and we have commented on a number of the initiatives that the administration has set forth. We've also been active in following patent developments within the People's Republic of China. We have commented directly to the government of China on a number of their initiatives, for example, the implementing regulations of the Chinese patent law and their revision of rules on patents and national standards.

We've also met with numerous delegations from China including from the patent office and from the trademark office.

Intellectual property is the engine of innovation, and it's not just within the United States and its major trading partners, but also within countries of emerging economies such as China, countries which are becoming, especially in the field of green technology, technology innovators and producers and not just technology consumers.

U.S.-China IP relations with respect to green technology must be built on this well-established and solid foundation of intellectual property.

There are a number of governments around the world, including our own, that have taken some very significant steps with respect to patents and green technologies. In the United States, the U.S. Patent and Trademark Office has initiated a pilot program for green technologies, which accelerates the examination of patent applications for green technology so that they can be issued sooner and so that the owners of that technology can put them on the market more quickly.

AIPLA has supported that initiative and we've actually asked that it be extended more widely to additional applications that it doesn't cover right now.

In addition, this month, the USPTO will co-host along with AIPLA and the World Intellectual Property Organization a World IP Day celebration on Capitol Hill that will focus on IP and green technology. And we expect that USPTO Director Kappos will outline the Office's ongoing strategy with respect to green technology.

Other major trading partners, such as the European Union, have put a lot of energy and effort into this. They've just issued a major study on patents on green technology. The European Patent Office has been involved in this as well.

However, we are not aware of any major initiatives that are coming out of the Chinese government, in particular, out of the patent office in China, that relate to ways to facilitate the patent protection, of green technology. But we think this is a fully ripe area of discussion for further development, and we think that is an appropriate topic for the U.S. government to discuss with the government of China because it would be to their benefit as well as to the benefit of technology producers in the United States as well.

There are a number of international treaties that relate to patenting. The main treaty is the World Trade Organization Agreement on Trade Related Aspects of Intellectual Property Rights, which is normally referred to as TRIPS. However, TRIPS is, in principle, technology neutral. It has a provision that prohibits discrimination based on the field of technology. Therefore, the principles are meant to be applied equally to all fields of technology, including green technology.

However, there are some cases where the members of the World Trade Organization have deviated from that, most notably recently in the area of pharmaceuticals and of medicines that are directed towards diseases that disproportionately affect developing countries. We don't believe that this type of an approach would be appropriate for green technology because it's a very different situation.

The breadth of technologies that are involved with green technologies, the diversity of innovators and developers, the availability of alternative technologies, and often the need for highly developed infrastructure and engineering know-how, are things that do not permit a simple solution with respect to green technologies.

Within the WTO, there's been a proposal for an Environmental Goods and Services Agreement that would reduce tariffs and non-tariff barriers, and we would say simply that this should not be done at the cost of provisions that would weaken intellectual property rights, in particular, the addition of compulsory licenses or limitations or exclusions from patentability. We believe that these are counterproductive measures even though they've been raised in a number of fora.

The most important forum in which they've been raised recently, which we've already discussed at length, is the UNFCCC, the United Nations Framework Convention on Climate Change. AIPLA was represented at the meeting in Copenhagen in December, and we were following very carefully the discussions on intellectual property rights and patent rights in particular.

We were dismayed that some of the proposals by the member states were actually directed not only towards compulsory licenses, but also towards exclusions from patent ability for future inventions on green technology, and the worst case was the invalidation of all existing patents on green technology in developing countries.

Fortunately, this did not end up in the final Copenhagen Accord. We believe that the Copenhagen Accord struck a good balance. It focuses on the need for stimulating technology transfer of green technology. It would set up a technology center to facilitate this, but it does not discuss intellectual property provisions, and it does not discuss any exclusions or exceptions for intellectual property, and we believe that this is the right approach and should continue to be the right approach as the U.S. goes forward with its discussions, both bilaterally and multilaterally.

I will say that the documents from Copenhagen that had these provisions are still on the table in the discussions of the UNFCCC. They will again be presented to the member states because, in fact, in December, there was not time for the member states to throw them out because everything was done at the last minute.

So we're hoping that those will not be revived, and the discussions will not go in that direction.

We believe that there is great potential for new cooperation, and we are just at the beginning of international cooperation in this area. We think that there are two areas in particular of cooperation. The first, of course, with respect to patents, is innovation and the development of technology; and the second, which is just as important, is the diffusion of technology, meaning the movement of technology across borders from one country to another, which is critical to solve this global problem. And I'd be very happy to discuss this more at length during the question and answer session.

Thank you.

[The statement follows:][8]

---

[8] Click here to read the prepared statement of Mr. Albert Tramposch

PANEL IV: Discussion, Questions and Answers

HEARING CO-CHAIR REINSCH: Okay. Thank you very much, all three of you.

Commissioner Fiedler, you want to begin.

COMMISSIONER FIEDLER: Mr. Bracy, there's a couple of things that you said that interest me. One, IP insurance. Let me see if I'm understanding how it operates, even though you didn't explain it completely. I buy insurance. I own intellectual property. I buy insurance to protect it. Somebody steals it. The insurance company pays me. If I prove it to whom?

MR. BRACY: Insurance is an arcane art from my point of view, but let me give you the political concept. One, yes, you buy insurance. The key thought here is that insurance is backed by the full faith and credit of the two governments. So if someone steals your intellectual property, they're stealing from the governments of China and the United States, and that makes a difference.

Now, as to how you value the intellectual property and how it's paid out, that's something that we've got some very smart people at Aon Insurance and some attorneys looking at to try to figure out. It's not a trivial exercise, but we think the most important thing is to send that confidence to the market that this matters, and if you're stealing intellectual property, you're stealing it from the governments.

Secondly, there's an ASCAP kind of registration component of this so that you're on a system that's jointly maintained by the two countries, and there would be some enforcement education arm that would be funded by these fees.

COMMISSIONER FIEDLER: And then I want to make sure I understand. You made a reference to Hong Kong and its legal system. So you're talking about adjudicating intellectual property disputes in Hong Kong.

MR. BRACY: Well, this is a very early thought.

COMMISSIONER FIEDLER: Let me finish the question.

MR. BRACY: Oh, sure.

COMMISSIONER FIEDLER: By contract. In other words, within contract provisions between people doing business together?

MR. BRACY: Let me tell you as far as we thought about it, and we don't claim that we're there, but I gave a speech at AmCham Hong Kong a couple of weeks ago, and this came up. Today, there are working systems where the IP is, in effect, in a lockbox under the Hong

Kong rule of law, and the manufacturing occurs in Shenzhen, which gives a lot more confidence to the market, and I heard encouraging things about it.

It makes me think that if we created such a joint entity, kind of a PICC/Export-Import entity, that maybe Hong Kong is the right place to put that.

COMMISSIONER FIEDLER: If the Chinese were to agree to that, would they not be acknowledging that they cannot protect intellectual property?

MR. BRACY: I think what we would pose is this is a game-changer. This is a new way of looking at it. We're not accusing anybody of anything. We're saying we have the same interests in protecting intellectual property. China is the largest exporter of solar, of wind, of LED. It's going to soon own a lot of the nuclear technology in the world because it's building more than anyone. We see an innate interest of China to find a way to give market confidence to grow that.

COMMISSIONER FIEDLER: Thank you.

Mr. Sumner, could you give us a quick education on emission levels of coal? So let's just take, for example, steelmaking coal that you're talking about that we mine here in the United States, and it's also shipped to the Chinese. What's the level of emissions now? And you say that the joint project you're working on with China will seriously reduce those emissions. So give us an example of what the projection is.

MR. SUMNER: Sure. The emissions data that I have, Commissioner, is not specific to steelmaking or anything of that nature. But I do have some statistics with me about the overall emissions, carbon emissions by the United States and by China.

COMMISSIONER FIEDLER: Is it coal related?

MR. SUMNER: I just have the overall statistics for those. I could certainly in later written material submit to you an analysis of the emissions from steelmaking and from--

COMMISSIONER FIEDLER: Well, I don't care about steelmaking. I was just thinking you're a coal company so you'd know what the emissions level were on coal.

MR. SUMNER: Yes. The exact numbers, unfortunately, I don't have, and I can't provide right now, but I would be happy to supply that information to you later.

COMMISSIONER FIEDLER: All right. Thank you.

HEARING CO-CHAIR REINSCH: Commissioner Cleveland.

COMMISSIONER CLEVELAND: Thank you.

Mr. Sumner, I spent 16 years in a former life working for the senior Senator from Kentucky so there are days when I used to think coal slurry went through my veins rather than blood.

MR. SUMNER: Sure.

COMMISSIONER CLEVELAND: So I ask this question with all due deference and appreciation of your industry. I think it's building a little bit on Jeff's question. How do you, as a company, experience the balancing act that goes on between environmental safeguards and economic growth? You seem to be right at the nexus of that in terms of Chinese policy.

MR. SUMNER: Sure. I think you mentioned two of the three E's that our Chairman, Greg Boyce, talks about--the need for energy to power the world's economies; the need for economic solutions; and the need for environmental solutions--the three E's.

And so as a company, obviously we're trying to provide coal to an expanding global world. We're doing it in the United State; we're doing that in Australia; we're doing that through our export platform in Australia. And now we hope in China to do something new, and that is to be the first foreign company to develop large-scale open-cut or surface mines in China to serve the growing market.

In China, about 90 percent or more, probably more, of the coal is mined by underground mining methods. So the Chinese, in spite of some of the recent safety horrible tragedies, they do some very fine underground mines, particularly in the southern part of Inner Mongolia. However, there are geological conditions, which are suitable for open-cut mining, where the Chinese because of their experience will mine via underground mining methods.

So we hope to bring our technology and our processes from the Powder River Basin in Wyoming to China. That's what we hope to do.

COMMISSIONER CLEVELAND: Okay.

MR. SUMNER: I'm sorry, Commissioner, but at the same time then, obviously, the environmental issue is critical, and so the world's economies in China and India--and I had the privilege of being in both countries last week. I'm a little bit jet-lagged this week frankly. But they are growing at incredible pace, and what's happened in China over the last 20 years, I will tell you, is just about to happen in India. It's absolutely incredible the increase in coal use that the Minister of State for Coal is projecting from now until 2030.

India generally consumes somewhere in the neighborhood of 600 million tons of coal per year. He sees that going to two billion tons of coal by 2030. Even in China, over the next ten years, China will add the equivalent of a full United States' year's worth of coal production to their production base over the next ten years. So we have to have a solution to the environmental issues. That's why we're trying to promote the development of clean coal technologies as rapidly as we can.

COMMISSIONER CLEVELAND: I was going to say while I might welcome that, I think some of my colleagues might be concerned by some of those statistics that you just mentioned.

Can you talk a little bit about the IGCC project which I think--

MR. SUMNER: Sure.

COMMISSIONER CLEVELAND: --sounds pretty exciting. When will it actually yield real results in terms of--

MR. SUMNER: First power is scheduled for next year. The first 250 megawatt IGCC unit is projected to be commissioned in 2011.

COMMISSIONER CLEVELAND: And do you see an acceleration of the use of IGCC after that? I mean there's always that pilot project, but how do you see that progressing?

MR. SUMNER: Well, I think it depends on how GreenGen goes obviously, but it probably will be the fifth IGCC power plant in the world once it's commissioned starting next year.

COMMISSIONER CLEVELAND: It's got a bumpy track record.

MR. SUMNER: Yes, but I think as it gets going, it will be, potentially, the model for clean coal around the world. The Chinese are building it very rapidly, and it's advancing at a great pace.

COMMISSIONER CLEVELAND: And the Chinese have financed that, or how has it been financed?

MR. SUMNER: Peabody has a six percent interest in the project under the joint venture agreement. So it's going to be supported by the major Chinese power companies, China Huaneng Group is the majority partner. And then several other Chinese companies like Guodian and Huadian and China Shenhua and China Coal also have a six percent interest like Peabody.

COMMISSIONER CLEVELAND: Thank you.

HEARING CO-CHAIR REINSCH: Thank you.

Commissioner Shea.

HEARING CO-CHAIR SHEA: I want to thank all three of you for being here. Appreciate your testimony.

First question is for Mr. Bracy. I know that your forum has developed eight separate initiatives, and I was wondering if you could explain to me how those initiatives dovetail with what President Obama and Hu Jintao agreed to in November? Are you working with the government of the United States and the government of China on those initiatives?

The second question I have is also for you. One of your initiatives is to create Strategic Energy Zones to facilitate innovation in the clean air energy area. Is there such a thing as a Strategic Energy Zone in the United States or in China, and do you see that? If not, do you see them coming on line at some point?

And then I have a question for Mr. Sumner after that.

MR. BRACY: Thank you, Commissioner Shea.

We did create eight initiatives. Six of them were embodied in the presidential agreement. So we felt pretty good about that, and David Sandalow has been very kind about giving us some credit for working out the hard language, and I would point out, we didn't just make recommendations and throw them over the transom. This was word-by-word negotiations with our Chinese counterparts, and they vetted it all the way up to the State Council. So I hope we helped the process.

The only two not included in that, one of them was the special energy zones, but not for lack of interest. We've modeled that on China's very exceptionally successful Special Economic Zones, like Shenzhen and so on.

The point is if you can concentrate resources investment and have an asterisk on policy, if you don't have to argue every national policy and say let's try this, let's try this, let's try this, then you can within that zone do things much more quickly and innovatively. If it doesn't work, it doesn't work.

The Chinese like that, but what they said was we want to pair up with you guys. So we don't want to just do it on our side; we want you to do it on your side. And there are earlier things the U.S. agreed to. When Secretary Paulson was running the SED last year, they created at the end of the term eight so-called "eco-partnerships," and those were a good idea, but there was no funding and no structure.

The Chinese are very anxious to do it. Our idea is that these special energy zones might be sort of Web 2.0 version of those eco-partnerships. Instead of Chongqing, population 30 million, cooperating with Denver, population two million, maybe we have three communities on each side, and each take a piece of the action and share it intensively and have people going back and forth.

HEARING CO-CHAIR SHEA: But this is just sort of a concept as opposed to anything being operationalized?

MR. BRACY: It's not, but the Chinese remain very active. We're talking with Dalian and Seattle and San Francisco and Shanghai and Changsha in southern China about a partnership, and I think it's going to take a little while to stand it up, about a year, but I think it has tremendous potential.

Now, on the China side, everywhere in China, there are low carbon zones, and small towns, large towns, everybody wants to be the low carbon king in China, and I don't quite get it. It's a fever. It really is a fever, but it's real; it's palpable.

HEARING CO-CHAIR SHEA: This is just a follow-up to

Commissioner Cleveland's question. As I heard your testimony, Peabody didn't have that much of a relationship with the Chinese market. You certainly don't have any mines in China, but you sold coal from your Australian operations to the Chinese market. Is that generally correct?

MR. SUMNER: Just in the last year we've begun doing that.

HEARING CO-CHAIR SHEA: So it's a relatively recent phenomenon. Describe the decision-making process within your company to enter into the GreenGen project. It doesn't sound like you had a lot of experience working with the Chinese, and I assume they invited you to participate and have an equity interest in this, in the GreenGen project.

How did you assess the offer and what types of concerns went through the corporate mind of Peabody?

MR. SUMNER: Sure. First of all, the relationship with China Huaneng, and Huaneng was our original point of entry into this project because China Huaneng is a member of the FutureGen Alliance for the FutureGen project in the United States so we got to know Huaneng through FutureGen. That was the initial introduction to the project.

It looked to us as a great opportunity. Then the invitation was extended to us to participate, and it looked to us to a wonderful opportunity to be a part of a signature clean energy project in the world. So it's not a major game-changing type investment for our company.

HEARING CO-CHAIR SHEA: Right.

MR. SUMNER: As I mentioned to Commissioner Cleveland, it's a six percent stake in the venture.

But I think it signifies something more important, and that is the need for collaboration in the area of coal and clean coal technologies between the United States and China.

So I think it's interesting, you're right, we don't have a mine yet in China. We're in the process of trying to develop, as I mentioned, large-scale open-cut mines. Looks like we may be headed towards Xinjiang in western China where the geology is suitable for that type of operation or Inner Mongolia. Those are probably the two areas where our first mines will be located.

We're also trying to develop a large coal mine, maybe the world's largest coal mine eventually, in Mongolia in the southern Gobi desert. So, obviously, Mongolia is a land-locked country. We're working very closely with the government of Mongolia to be a strategic partner, but China is the market.

HEARING CO-CHAIR SHEA: Thank you.

MR. SUMNER: Thank you, Commissioner Shea.

HEARING CO-CHAIR REINSCH: Thank you.

Commissioner Videnieks.

COMMISSIONER VIDENIEKS: Good afternoon, gentlemen. A quick question to you, a couple questions to Mr. Sumner. Do I understand correctly that open-pit--how would you classify? Is that surface mining or sub-surface?

MR. SUMNER: Surface, yes.

COMMISSIONER VIDENIEKS: So you're basically saying the sub-surface mining is 99 percent in PRC?

MR. SUMNER: It's greater than 90 percent, Commissioner.

COMMISSIONER VIDENIEKS: Greater than 90.

MR. SUMNER: That is correct.

COMMISSIONER VIDENIEKS: Okay. So I was wondering, of surface mining, what proportion would you say is mountain top removal or do they have it over there?

MR. SUMNER: That's a question that I don't know the answer to.

COMMISSIONER VIDENIEKS: If you do find out, can you please send it to us--the information?

MR. SUMNER: Sure. Sure. Absolutely.

COMMISSIONER VIDENIEKS: Newspapers have referred to other coal company leaders as saying that violations are a cost of doing business, and you stated that safety is the paramount objective, above profit, was my understanding.

Does Peabody differ a lot from other companies, stands by itself, or do I understand things wrongly?

MR. SUMNER: We do. And thank you for your question. In my opinion, when Mr. Boyce came to Peabody, his major focus, Commissioner, was instilling the value of safety in our organization, and that's from the top down. In fact, this is one of the few meetings that I've attended where it didn't begin with a safety contact.

Typically, a meeting, whether it's at the mines or at our headquarters in St. Louis,, begins with a safety contact, and here a good safety contact might be, if we had to evacuate the Dirksen Building, where would we go, and that sort of thing? And we do that type of thing as routine practice in our company.

In the wake of the accidents that have happened in the last couple of days, Mr. Boyce sent a note out, and I'll just read a quick sentence from it:

To all 7,300 Peabody employees: Be relentless in your focus to achieve zero incidents of any kind.

COMMISSIONER VIDENIEKS: What is your violations record? The record as described in the newspapers in West Virginia, the violation record was huge, a huge number of contested or unresolved citations. Does Peabody stand alone being fairly clean on this issue, safety being the paramount objective?

MR. SUMNER: Thank you for the question, Commissioner.

We do not operate mines in West Virginia so we participate in the Illinois Basin.

COMMISSIONER VIDENIEKS: In the United States?

MR. SUMNER: Right. But we have the industry leading safety record, and I would just very quickly go into a statistic for you: not only do we lead the industry in terms of safety performance, the lowest incident rate in the industry, but if you look at our safety statistics in comparison to other industries, it's safer to work in a Peabody coal mine than work in the utility industry, wholesale--

COMMISSIONER VIDENIEKS: Per what unit? Per dollar of output? Or how do you measure this?

MR. SUMNER: We measure it in terms of incidents per 200,000--

COMMISSIONER VIDENIEKS: Per employee, per 1,000 employees, how?

MR. SUMNER: --per 200,000 hours worked, and that's the standard for OSHA.

COMMISSIONER VIDENIEKS: All right. One more question. We had prior testimony a year or so ago by the governor of Montana who stated that one of the impediments to clean coal technology is different laws in different states. Would you agree with that? We've got to make recommendations to Congress as to areas.

MR. SUMNER: Sure. Thank you for your question again.

And we agree with that 100 percent. That was one of the issues that Peabody raised with respect to the Waxman-Markey legislation, that it did not contain an enabling framework for carbon capture and storage deployment at a broad scale in the United States, and that's one of the issues that was omitted.

COMMISSIONER VIDENIEKS: Maybe you could send in some suggested language, which we could analyze here and see whether it could be further--

MR. SUMNER: Sure. Thank you very much.

COMMISSIONER VIDENIEKS: Thank you, sir. My time is running out.

HEARING CO-CHAIR REINSCH: Thank you.

Commissioner Wessel.

COMMISSIONER WESSEL: Thank you and I apologize for being a couple of minutes late so I apologize if my questions have already been answered.

But I want to talk about the issue of intellectual property enforcement as it relates to some of these clean and green technologies.

Do you think Section 337 has utility in this area? I don't remember seeing any 337 actions regarding these products. Are we seeing imbedded IP in terms of violations being imported into the United States already?

MR. TRAMPOSCH: Thank you, Commissioner.

As I said, most intellectual property is technology neutral so the same rules would apply under Section 337 to green technology as to any other technology, and I would say that the utilization of Section 337 would parallel both the amount of imports and the value of the imports. I'm not aware of any particular cases that involve green technology although I'm sure that there must be some because many of the cases get settled.

COMMISSIONER WESSEL: Right.

MR. TRAMPOSCH: That's one of the advantages of Section 337, is it's very fast, not just in the proceedings, but because they're very often settled and so the case is finished very quickly, and sometimes they're not, it's before they become public.

COMMISSIONER WESSEL: And a probably more effective remedy than exists in most other areas of trade.

MR. TRAMPOSCH: Exactly. And I think that that's the way it's designed so it works very well.

But my guess is that as green technology becomes more and more utilized, as the market grows, as the value grows, and as more products are imported, then Section 337 will be a very important and very effective remedy in this area for U.S. intellectual property holders.

COMMISSIONER WESSEL: And Mr. Bracy, and I apologize, again, for not having been here for the discussion you had about the insurance approach, and what I may ask, again, you've already answered or maybe embodied in the idea you were proposing or discussing.

When we confronted the recall and product liability issues a couple of years ago, one of the free-market private sector approaches that was suggested, which doesn't usually come out of my mouth, was trying to have liability insurance regarding those products issued or purchased by importers of record, where you would have private sector insurers who would determine what the actuarial rates are.

MR. BRACY: Uh-huh.

COMMISSIONER WESSEL: And clearly at that point with product liability issues, one would assume that an import of a pin from Great Britain would probably have a lower actuarial rate of concern than a product coming from China because of the safety regimes, et cetera.

But that the lack of transparency in the Chinese market hopefully could be overcome by U.S. insurers and importers demanding access to be able to look at supply chains, et cetera. I think this potentially could have some utility in the IP area, that if we were to have IP insurance for clean and green and maybe all other products related to imbedded IP, that if the importer of record had to get IP insurance, that the private sector may do a better job of looking at supply chains and being able to investigate and get transparency.

Can you give me your first impressions of that, of whether that kind of approach rather than what I heard you say, which is the U.S. and the Chinese having to provide the reserves, et cetera, at the top end, where you get into political problems? But, by creating this economic incentive for transparency through the private sector, you might be able to get greater IP protections over time?

MR. BRACY: Well, Commissioner, thanks.

I think the key is to try to some new things. If we just point fingers and have the same old conversation, that doesn't get us very far. I would argue that things are different as China emerges as the leading international exporter of a lot of these technologies.

So I think that has bearing. I've heard people say let's tie it to financing rates. We always envisioned, by the way, not some government bureaucracy doing it, but they would subcontract it to insurance companies who are specialists in this, but that thought, I still think is important.

China showed during the Olympics and they're showing during Shanghai Expo now that if they care about intellectual property, they can protect it, and people generally don't fool around with it. So--

COMMISSIONER WESSEL: I think if the importers here cared about it and had their money on the line for IP violations, the actuarial rates might actually stimulate greater protection.

Mr. Tramposch.

MR. TRAMPOSCH: Yes, thank you.

There's actually an interesting difference between the Chinese enforcement system and the U.S. enforcement system on IP, and that is that China actually has government agencies that will investigate infringements of intellectual property, whereas, in the United States, with very few exceptions, it's a private action. And the advantage of insurance is that the private actions are extremely expensive, they can cost up to millions of dollars just for lawyers' fees, and it's really beyond the reach of many small or medium-sized enterprises.

And the insurance that I've heard about before, and I think what I've heard about may be a little bit different than what you're looking at, and what you're looking at sounds actually very interesting, but it's intended to help small and medium-sized enterprises be able to fight an infringement suit against a larger company without going broke.

And very often, an action can be decided by whose money will last the longest, and when your money runs out, then you settle.

COMMISSIONER WESSEL: But if as a matter of law, an importer of record had to have the IP insurance presumably that would treat everyone the same, the small, medium, large-sized importers, and create much more transparency and protection in the system; wouldn't it?

MR. TRAMPOSCH: I think that's possible, but I'd have to look at the details a little bit more. There is a Customs registration system for copyright and for trademarks but not for patents. It's the 337 actions that are used for patents, and of course, those are also very expensive, sometimes more expensive because they're so quick.

So some alternative to that that would at least help small/medium-sized enterprises, I think it would be worthwhile to look at.

COMMISSIONER WESSEL: Thank you.

HEARING CO-CHAIR REINSCH: Thank you.

Commissioner Bartholomew.

VICE CHAIR BARTHOLOMEW: Thanks very much and thank you to all of our witnesses. It's an interesting discussion.

Mr. Bracy and Mr. Tramposch, I'd like your observations. This concept of a lockbox in Hong Kong--I guess there are two sets of questions. One is Hong Kong is changing now that the handover has been consolidated, what--ten years now.

Last year, when we were in Hong Kong after having been in China on business, my room and the room of one of my colleagues was searched in Hong Kong while we were dining with somebody who is not what I would call a most-favored person of the Chinese government. What do you think about the safety and sanctity of IP if it's held in a lockbox in Hong Kong?

Let me just put the other piece of it out there, which is that certainly some of the IP theft that has been taking place has been taking place by state-owned or state-controlled companies in China. The Chinese have had a pattern of forced tech transfer, and now with their indigenous innovations program, what incentive would the Chinese government have to ensure the sanctity of IP that was being held in that lockbox? I presume most of that would be Western IP.

And then the second piece of it is what confidence is there that in Hong Kong that the sanctity would be maintained?

MR. BRACY: I'm going to do some freewheeling here. We don't have all these things figured out, and by the way, anybody who has ideas in this arena, please join the party. We're a bunch of volunteers who are trying to figure some things out and trying to bring the best minds together to come up with some new solutions.

Hong Kong, I think, in my view, first of all--IP isn't just a widget increasingly. Companies are building things in open systems and publishing because they want other people to connect to it.

Secondly, the Hong Kong notion is mainly a notion to give confidence to the market that their property will be protected, and I think Hong Kong offers real advantages there. Nothing is perfect that I'm aware of, but I think people feel a sense of comfort in the British-based system of law in Hong Kong.

I do think China has a stake and understands the stake in protecting intellectual property. We may not like the current version of the indigenous innovation and most of us don't. We'll see how it comes out, but I think that actually shows that China is trying to grow its intellectual property, and it puts great value in intellectual property. I think they're pretty wise about that.

What I'm hoping to do is get some new ideas and try some new things in this limited area. The clean energy zone is a bubble of cooperation. I lived through the chill of the last few months in Beijing of bilateral relations, which is coming out now. I think we're thawing. But clean energy was never touched by that. The Chinese really want to cooperate.

So we see this as an opportunity about clean energy, but if we find some workable solutions, whatever those are, patent pool, lockbox, IP insurance, then those can be expanded more broadly as China becomes more and more of a world player.

VICE CHAIR BARTHOLOMEW: Mr. Tramposch.

MR. TRAMPOSCH: Yes, thanks.

I agree with Dennis in a lot of what he said. In the last 20, 30 years, as intellectual property has become more universally accepted around the world, and as recognized by the TRIPS Agreement, it's not enough just to obtain intellectual property rights. What's really important is the ability to enforce.

Years ago, the Soviet Union had a very, very modern patent law, and anyone from around the world could get a patent on the same terms that they would in their home country. The problem was there was no way you could enforce it so it really wasn't really worth much.

There have been difficulties in China, partly from the things that you mentioned. Also, the difficulties of a foreign company actually suing in China and using the legal system, and these are things either perceived or real.

I think that the concept of using Hong Kong and the Hong Kong legal system is meant, as Dennis pointed out, to increase the level of confidence in the legal system of China so that it would encourage the importation of technology.

There are two things that are necessary for bringing technology in. You need to have the funding for it, but you also need to have a stable and reliable legal system, regulations and enforcement, in the country, so that you can get your investment out. Intellectual property stimulates innovation, but it really stimulates investment, and if there is no way to get a return on the investment, as Commissioner Wessel has pointed out earlier today, then there simply won't be any technology transfer.

VICE CHAIR BARTHOLOMEW: But if I understand this correctly, this would be ultimately encouraging the production of clean energy technology in China based on U.S. patents. Is that underlying what you're envisioning here?

MR. BRACY: No, I think we see--some very smart people have told me, first of all, you don't have to even sell your product in any given market to have it pirated. If it's anywhere in the world, people can presumably reverse engineer it.

But smart people--Applied Materials of California is one of our key members, and they sell a whole system, and, yes, it is equipment, but it's a whole bunch of know-how. IGCC plants are the same thing. It isn't just pieces and parts; it's know-how.

So we see this as a collaborative thing. I don't see it just as U.S. technology going into China, but increasingly Huaneng is licensing technology to the U.S. ENN is licensing technology to the FutureGen project.

VICE CHAIR BARTHOLOMEW: And do the Chinese have concerns that their technology is going to be ripped off by the United States?

MR. BRACY: Absolutely. Any company that owns intellectual property, and they put it on slide two of their PowerPoint, that's their asset. They're publicly traded entities who are protecting their shareholder value, and their shareholder value is locked up in their patents and their intellectual property.

Any company that wants to defend its wealth is going to try to protect its intellectual property in worldwide markets.

HEARING CO-CHAIR SHEA: Thank you.

Commissioner Mulloy.

COMMISSIONER MULLOY: Thank you, Mr. Chairman.

First, just to Mr. Sumner. As a fellow who grew up in the anthracite coal fields of Pennsylvania, we now call it Joe Biden country, we were taught that anthracite is a cleaner-burning coal or hard coal. Anthracite coal is cleaner burning and less polluting than bituminous coal, which we associated with Pittsburgh and Kentucky.

HEARING CO-CHAIR REINSCH: Now be careful where you're

going with this.

COMMISSIONER MULLOY: Is that correct?

MR. SUMNER: Unfortunately, I'm not an expert in anthracite coals, Commissioner. We do not participate in the market in Pennsylvania.

COMMISSIONER MULLOY: Okay.

MR. SUMNER: In western Pennsylvania. I'd be happy to talk to some of my technical colleagues in our geology or engineering department and get you the answer.

COMMISSIONER MULLOY: Is most of the coal in China bituminous coal?

MR. SUMNER: We're still trying to find out. We don't know the answer to that question, but some of the coal reserves that we're looking at are both sub-bituminous as well as bituminous.

COMMISSIONER MULLOY: I never knew India had a lot of coal.

MR. SUMNER: Yes, they do.

COMMISSIONER MULLOY: And is it bituminous as well?

MR. SUMNER: My understanding is that that is correct.

COMMISSIONER MULLOY: That's interesting. So the potential pollution problem is enormous?

MR. SUMNER: Right. And Commissioner, the issue in India, the reason why India is so interested in supplies of coal from other countries is because their coal is known for its high ash content.

COMMISSIONER MULLOY: I see.

Well, I have a question for Mr. Bracy. One, I see that you've been working with my old boss Norm Mineta, who I always liked very much. He was terrific.

MR. BRACY: I love Norm.

COMMISSIONER MULLOY: In the study, that was done for the National Foreign Trade Council by the Dewey LeBoeuf law firm, which we talked about this morning. Were you here when that discussion was going on?

MR. BRACY: I was not, Commissioner.

COMMISSIONER MULLOY: Okay. This study says that China has a government policy that no wind farm can be constructed in China that doesn't meet a 70 percent local content requirement. And the effect of this is to reduce the ability of foreigners to sell into China.

But the second thing it does is it induces foreign companies then to relocate in China to be able to meet that domestic content requirement. Okay.

MR. BRACY: Okay.

COMMISSIONER MULLOY: Do you accept that?

MR. BRACY: Well, in rough terms. My understanding is Gary Locke, Secretary of Commerce, at the last JCCT meeting, the Joint Committee on Commerce and Trade actually negotiated most of the local content rules away. I'm not an expert on that, but that was one of their primary objectives in this last round of the JCCT.

COMMISSIONER MULLOY: Yes. I think it was raised there. I'm not sure it was resolved.

MR. BRACY: Well, they announced an agreement. I can't quote what it was.

COMMISSIONER MULLOY: Okay. Well, if they haven't, in your testimony you say, "Both the U.S. and China currently impose import tariffs on a wide variety of clean energy technologies." I would expect that would be wind turbines and other things.

MR. BRACY: For solar panels we just raised it to 2.5 percent from last, on a Customs finding.

COMMISSIONER MULLOY: You say "China is now the largest exporter of many of these clean energy technologies," and I would expect that because they have a policy, a national industrial policy, to develop them, and that they "would benefit from the lowering or removal of tariffs" on our part. Right.

What would be the impact on domestic producers of those clean energy technologies here in the United States if we followed that policy recommendation?

MR. BRACY: Remember, it would go both ways. And it would not be just wind turbines, but it would be the whole series of things. Chinese inbound tariffs can be up to 35 percent. Ours tend to be in the single digits. China has recently, I was told by the NDRC, completed their ASEAN negotiations, and they took tariffs off clean energy or they are under the ASEAN regime.

So we believe it's a new day in China. Five years ago, I would never have said this, maybe even three years ago, but now that they're the largest exporter of these goods and services, they stand to benefit from a world market without tariffs.

We haven't been able to do that under a WTO framework. That multilateral thing has gotten in the way. We're saying let's do it bilaterally first, and maybe the world will follow, that not only will increase commerce both directions, but it will also bring down the cost of clean energy as we try and grapple with developing countries getting access to clean energy.

COMMISSIONER MULLOY: Okay.

HEARING CO-CHAIR REINSCH: Thank you.

COMMISSIONER MULLOY: Thank you.

HEARING CO-CHAIR REINSCH: Mr. Tramposch, I thought I

heard you say in your testimony or suggest that EGSA might somehow compromise intellectual property rights. Could you elaborate on that?

MR. TRAMPOSCH: I'm sorry, sir, that?

HEARING CO-CHAIR REINSCH: That EGSA, an Environmental Goods and Services Agreement, might compromise IP rights. Can you explain that a little bit more?

MR. TRAMPOSCH: What I was saying is that it should not be negotiated so that it does compromise IP rights. And part of my reason for saying that is because of the current climate of multilateral negotiations where any time anything involving technology is discussed, then there's a group of developing countries that bring in the desire for compulsory licenses or exclusions from patentability. That's happened at WTO before. It's happened at the WHO in respect to medicines, and most recently it happened in the UNFCCC.

So my statement was that we should not look to the weakening of intellectual property rights as any sort of a bargaining chip that can be given away in order to obtain other benefits such as reduction of tariffs, import tariffs.

HEARING CO-CHAIR REINSCH: Okay. Right. I don't think anybody here would disagree with that, and that actually leads to my other question, but, first, to follow up, do you have any sense that the United States government might be contemplating that in its advocacy of an EGSA?

MR. TRAMPOSCH: Not particularly in that case, but in the case of the UNFCCC, while the State Department took a very strong stand that we agreed with, that intellectual property should not be negotiated, in the lead-up to Copenhagen, there were some worries that there would be a compromise on the intellectual property provisions if it felt that an agreement in Copenhagen was important enough and that there was no other way to get it.

In fact, some of the European countries were weakening during the Copenhagen discussions so it's simply something that seems to arise in every forum, and we just feel like we need to raise our voice on this side. Not that we expect that the United States would take a different position. We like to raise our voice.

HEARING CO-CHAIR REINSCH: My sense has been that this is an important concern. I think you're making an important point, and I for one certainly agree with you. My sense has been in the last four months, five months, that some major developing country positions have been moving in our direction on that subject.

Would you agree with that or not? Not all the way, but in our direction.

MR. TRAMPOSCH: I think what has happened is that a number

of the studies that have come out that show that, especially in the area of green technology, that a large percentage of the new patents are coming from entities that reside in developing countries, somewhere around 30 percent, which is huge.

And those countries realize that if they weaken intellectual property with respect to green technology, they're really hurting themselves as much as helping themselves.

HEARING CO-CHAIR REINSCH: Once again proving the axiom that one really becomes interested in this subject when one has intellectual property of one's own to protect.

Well, good. Thank you very much.

COMMISSIONER WESSEL: Can I ask one clarifying question? To follow on what you just asked--

HEARING CO-CHAIR REINSCH: Commissioner Wessel has one question and Commissioner Mulloy has one question, and then we will stop.

COMMISSIONER WESSEL: My understanding then was that Todd Stern, our climate negotiator, originally was looking at the potential for compulsory licensing to be part of a deal, but that business and others have helped change it. So that it was on the table; is that correct?

MR. TRAMPOSCH: I don't have any personal knowledge of that. There were so many rumors going around, but we as the industry representatives--I was there on behalf of AIPLA, but I was on the International Chamber of Commerce delegation and part of what they call the BINGO, the Business and Industry NGOs.

We did not want to take any chances so we had daily briefings by the USTR. We had daily business briefings with the State Department. The State Department assured us that they were very solid, that they would not consider any modification on intellectual property. They did not want the provisions. They didn't want anything discussed in there even included in the text. But we met with them each day to make sure that they knew our position.

COMMISSIONER WESSEL: Okay. Thank you.

HEARING CO-CHAIR REINSCH: Commissioner Mulloy, the last question.

COMMISSIONER MULLOY: Thank you, Mr. Chairman, for this opportunity.

Mr. Tramposch, I was very interested when my colleague raised the Section 337 of our trade laws as a way to get at the intellectual property imports, the goods that violate intellectual property rights that are coming into the country.

Does that section of the law now permit the United States

government to self-initiate 337 proceedings? And if not, do you think it should?

MR. TRAMPOSCH: My understanding is that it needs to initiated by the holder of the intellectual property. It's a request to the ITC to initiate the investigation.

COMMISSIONER MULLOY: Right.

MR. TRAMPOSCH: My understanding is that there needs to be a request at this time.

COMMISSIONER MULLOY: You mentioned these are pretty expensive lawsuits. Do you think it would be useful if maybe the Justice Department had the authority to initiate a 337 lawsuit?

MR. TRAMPOSCH: As I mentioned earlier, it's a difference in principle without different systems acting, and in the U.S., traditionally, intellectual property is--

COMMISSIONER MULLOY: I understand.

MR. TRAMPOSCH: Protection is initiated by the owner of the intellectual property. We would be very interested in hearing about and discussing an alternative way the U.S.--

COMMISSIONER MULLOY: Would you take that back to your group and have them think about that, and then see what they think?

MR. TRAMPOSCH: I'd be happy to bring that back and give you any reactions that we have.

COMMISSIONER MULLOY: That would be terrific. Thank you.

HEARING CO-CHAIR REINSCH: Thank you and thank you very much to the panel. This has been very enlightening. I appreciate it, and with that, the hearing is adjourned.

[Whereupon, at 2:35 p.m., the hearing was adjourned.]

ADDITIONAL MATERIAL SUPPLIED FOR THE RECORD

Statement of Hon. Michelle J. DePass, Assistant Administrator for International Affairs, U.S. Environmental Protection Agency, Washington, D.C.[9]

---

[9] Click here to read the statement of the Honorable Michelle J. DePass

PUBLIC COMMENT SUBMITTED FOR THE RECORD

Submitted via email by Jean Public of Whitehouse Station,

New Jersey on May 20, 2010

"We need to cut out most trade with China. They are sending us poison after poison after poison. Their actions have cost many, many American companies to go out of business. The trade with China is hurting the United States. We need to make more products here in America. We have the right to do that. Stop all the ships coming from China to America. They are a very bad society, and kill people at the drop of a hat. They are also brutal to animals. We should not be relying on this country. Such reliance is extremely bad for America, which must make itself strong. If we don't, I see an end to America. We are pursuing very, very poor government policies these days. Cut the trade with China. Now."

www.ingramcontent.com/pod-product-compliance
Lightning Source LLC
Chambersburg PA
CBHW082136290526
45794CB00008B/3064